IMAGINE READING THIS BOOK

How Mental Pictures Influence Your Decisions

IMAGINE READING *THIS* BOOK

How Mental Pictures
Influence Your Decisions

NICK KOLENDA

Contents

Preface

WHY ARE YOU reading this sentence?

Seriously, retrace your steps. What prompted you to pick up this book? What brought you to this exact moment?

If you purchased this book, then you'll be investing time and money to read it. Clearly, *something* is motivating you.

Or, if you are previewing this book, what are you hoping to find as you scan these words? What would trigger that moment of decisiveness where you suddenly say, "What the heck, I'll buy it."

In both cases, you're probably generating conscious reasons: *I want to read this book because . . .*

. . . it seems interesting.

. . . it was on sale.

. . . I enjoyed his other books.

. . . my friend recommended it.

Pretty reasonable, right?

However, in this book, you'll discover that those reasons—the reasons that you *think* are driving your decisions—are wrong. You're not reading this book because of those reasons. You're reading this book because of a hidden mechanism that occurred below your conscious awareness, a devious mechanism that controls every decision in your life. Every decision across the world.

This book will reveal that mechanism. The following chapters will unravel the conscious reasons behind any decision, delving into the nonconscious roots that are *actually* controlling these decisions.

And we'll examine these decisions in the context of motivation. Tell me if this sounds familiar:

You glance at your daily schedule and notice an effortful task: study for midterms, run two miles, write your novel, *anything*. You *want* to do this task. You value the long-term benefits. But, for whatever reason, you don't possess the motivation. You just stare. And stare. And stare. And then, of course, watch Netflix . . . obviously you need a break from staring. But after a quick episode, it's back to the grind for—*erhm*—more staring.

So, why aren't you motivated? The answer is simple: You're targeting the wrong reasons. Your brain is targeting conscious reasons when it should be targeting the nonconscious mechanism. Unlike conscious reasons, these deeper roots give you control of the wheel so that you can harness and aim your behavior in the direction that you want.

And the best part? It doesn't take much effort. Contrary to popular belief, motivation doesn't require brute strength or willpower. You don't need to *endure* anything. An admirable feat? Sure. But you can achieve that feat in a simpler way: Just use this mechanism to instill a desire.

In other words, this book won't help you trudge through undesirable tasks; this book will transform undesirable tasks into something that you genuinely want to do. Something that doesn't feel effortful. Something that doesn't require willpower in the first place.

Plus, you can use this mechanism to motivate other people. Motivate your staff to hit their targets. Motivate your students to do their homework. Motivate your customers to buy. Motivate your kids to eat vegetables. *Motivate any decision in any context.*

I'm excited for our journey. Let's get started.

Introduction

TWO SECONDS AGO, your brain faced a decision: *Hmm, should I stop reading here? Or continue to the next page?*

And . . . here you are. So, what happened? How did you make this decision? How do you make *any* decision?

Here's the answer: You make decisions by "simulating" the outcome. A few seconds ago, you imagined yourself continuing to read this book. If this mental picture felt good, then you continued.

Each day, you face an endless barrage of similar decisions. *Hmm, should I . . .*

. . . eat this ice cream?

. . . go to the gym?

. . . buy this coat?

. . . study for chemistry?

. . . move to North Carolina?

Any decision, big or small, can be traced to a mental picture: You imagine the outcome, and then you judge the emotional response.

This process seems simple, perhaps even advantageous, but it has some hidden flaws that bias your decisions. The following chapters will help you overcome those flaws so that you can make better decisions, enabling you to make the right choices without succumbing to fleeting temptations. Think of this book as the instruction manual that failed to arrive with your brain.

In this book, we'll jump into a microscopic ship and venture deep inside the brain, traveling to the origin of these mental pictures. You often hear terms like "subconscious influence." This book will finally explain, in clear and precise language, what is occurring beneath the surface of every decision.

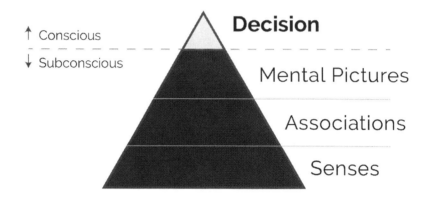

This book has three stages:

- ▶ **Stage 1: Mental Pictures.** You make decisions by imagining the outcome, and you confuse the vividness of this imagery for a desire: *Hmm, should I flip to the next page? I can easily picture myself flipping to the next page. Therefore, I must want to do it.* You can boost motivation by strengthening the clarity and vividness of these mental pictures.
- ▶ **Stage 2: Associations.** Your mental pictures depend on the associations in your brain. You can strengthen the clarity and vividness of mental pictures by targeting these associations.
- ▶ **Stage 3: Senses.** Every association in your brain is infused with sensory experience. These sensory elements breathe life into your mental pictures.

So, if you're ready, let's jump inside our ship and travel to these hidden depths. Our first stop? Mental pictures.

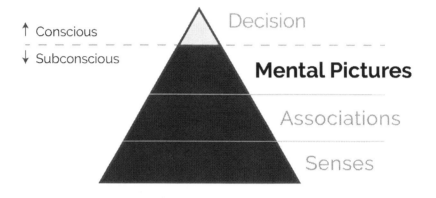

STAGE 1

Mental Pictures

LAST YEAR, I accidentally hit a child.

It felt like slow motion. While entering the small gym in my apartment building, I noticed a young boy—maybe 4 years old—appear from nowhere, placing himself in the direct path of the door.

BAM!

"Oh [*expletive*]," I thought, as the door collided with his head. I looked around. Nobody else was there. Panic flooded in.

As I bent down to check on him, we locked gazes. He said nothing, but his eyes communicated a clear confusion: *Is this painful or funny?* He was unsure how to react, and he was studying *me*, as if I were the keeper of this mystery.

I noticed his dilemma, and I took a risk. Instead of my natural instinct to show concern, I started laughing; I joined him on the floor and started acting goofy. To my relief, his confusion became laughter. He saw my reaction and concluded that the situation was funny (not painful). In the end, he was okay. No harm done.

Now, you might be quick to blame the child's confusion on his underdeveloped brain. Any adult, surely, can tell the difference between pain and humor, right? Not necessarily. In this part of the book, you'll discover that even you, a bona fide adult, can feel the same confusing mixture of emotions. And, much like the child, you make sense of your emotions by examining the context.

We can unravel this idea through a concept called *simulation fluency*. It sounds complicated, but it's really simple.

Let's start with fluency.

Fluency

Pop quiz. Is the following statement true or false?

Lima is in Peru

You probably noticed the weird font, right? This visual cue is irrelevant to the meaning of that statement, so any rational human being should remain unaffected by it.

The problem? We're not rational human beings. Researchers confirmed that, indeed, this statement seemed less truthful in a weird font (Reber & Schwarz, 1999).

And it's not just fonts. Statements also seem less truthful when spoken with heavy accents (Lev-Ari & Keysar, 2010).

In those contexts, you feel an ambiguous mixture of emotions related to cognitive difficulty: *Hmm, something about this statement feels weird and difficult.* Much like the confused young boy, you remain uncertain about the true nature of these vague feelings. You diagnose them by searching the context for a possible explanation—and, unfortunately, you often attribute these emotions to the wrong source: *Hmm, this statement feels weird and difficult. Therefore, this statement must be false.*

This effect isn't limited to random quizzes about geography; it can also influence vital decisions in your life. Perhaps you are sitting in your doctor's office, listening to important instructions about your health. You might instinctively dismiss this information if your doctor is speaking with an accent: *Hmm, why does this information feel difficult to process? It must be unimportant.* You might enact racist and prejudiced behaviors, while ignoring vital instructions about your health and well-being, merely due to the irrelevant traits of your doctor's voice.

And the perception of truth is merely one example. You derive *many* conclusions from ease or difficulty: *Hmm, this stimulus is easy to process. It must be:*

- ▶ **Easy.** Exercises seem easier to do when they are displayed in a simple font (e.g., 20 pushups vs. *20 pushups*). *Hmm, this feels easy to read. It must be easy to do.*
- ▶ **Close.** Cities seem closer when they are displayed in a simple font (e.g., Boston vs. *Boston*). *Hmm, this feels easy to read. It must be closer.*
- ▶ **Valuable.** Financial stocks seem more valuable when they are easy to pronounce (e.g., KAR vs. RDO). *Hmm, this stock feels right. It should perform well.*

(See Song & Schwarz, 2008; Alter & Oppenheimer, 2008; Alter & Oppenheimer, 2006.)

We've been discussing *processing fluency*, the ease or difficulty of processing information, but you find the same effects with *conceptual fluency*, when something pops into your mind very easily.

Suppose that you're standing in a liquor aisle, and you see two options for rum: Captain Morgan or Admiral Nelson. You decide to grab Captain Morgan; it's a little more expensive, but—what the heck—you feel an urge to buy it. You tell yourself that it will be more appealing for guests.

But wait, is that *really* why you bought it? Or, did you buy it because of the strange commercial that aired the night before? In that commercial, a captain walks into a crowded bar, while each person greets him with a polite, "Captain." By the end of the 30-second commercial, you hear "Captain" repeated 31 times.[1] Fast forward to the next day, while you debate the choice—Captain Morgan vs. Admiral Nelson—you feel a weird sensation about Captain Morgan. Something *feels* more familiar. Naturally, you derive this conclusion: *Hmm, Captain Morgan is entering my brain very easily. Therefore, I must want to buy it because [it'll be more appealing for guests].*

Oftentimes, your conscious reasons for buying a product are meaningless; these reasons can emerge *after* your brain has already made the decision. Many people downplay advertising because they never think: *Hmm, I want to buy Captain Morgan because they had a good commercial last night.* But usually, that's not the purpose of advertising. You don't need to be consciously persuaded; heck, you don't need to *remember* a commercial. Commercials are effective as long as they increase the fluency of a brand. If that brand pops into your mind, then you will do the heavy lifting: *you* will generate the conscious reason why you should buy it. Your brain should start earning commissions.

If anything, commercials are more effective if you *don't* remember them. If you remember a commercial, then your brain can explain the

---

[1] It's a real commercial. You can watch my YouTube video—The Psychology of Commercials—for details and other examples.

fluency: *Hmm, why is Captain Morgan entering my mind? Oh, it's because of their commercial.* Without this memory, your brain will need to search for an explanation: *Hmm, why is Captain Morgan entering my mind? Oh, I must want to buy it.*

Now that we've seen processing fluency and conceptual fluency, let's merge them into a third type: *simulation fluency.*

Simulation Fluency

Next time you pick up this book to continue reading, ask yourself: Why am I starting to read again?

Well, I'm bored—I need something to do.

Yes, but reading? Why not something else? And how did you know that reading would solve your boredom?

Your brain answered those questions by running a hypothetical simulation: You created a mental picture in which you were reading this book. This imagery helped you judge the emotional reaction.

Still with me?

So far, we've seen processing fluency: *Hmm, this statement is difficult to process. Therefore, it must be false.*

We've seen conceptual fluency: *Hmm, Captain Morgan is entering my mind very easily. Therefore, I must want to buy it.*

Now, let's merge these ideas into simulation fluency: *Hmm, I can easily picture myself reading this book. Therefore, I must want to read it.*

In other words: If you can easily and vividly picture yourself performing a behavior, you conclude that you must desire this behavior.

This mechanism is the hidden process behind every decision, including important decisions, like legal verdicts. Jurors use mental pictures to determine their verdicts: *Is he guilty? Hmm, based on the evidence, I can picture him committing this crime. Therefore, he must be guilty.*

Read that statement again, and look closely. Their verdict isn't based on the evidence; it's based on the mental picture. The evidence constructs their mental picture, but their final verdict is based on the vividness of this imagery.

But who cares, right? Wouldn't strong evidence create a strong mental picture? Aren't the conclusions the same? No—they're not. And that's why it matters. Many variables can influence these mental pictures (and thus the verdict) without being relevant to the evidence.

In January of 2020, disgraced movie producer Harvey Weinstein was on trial for egregious crimes of sexual assault. On his first day of trial, Weinstein walked—or rather, hobbled—into the courtroom with a walker, which he hadn't used before the trial. Whether or not he needed this walker is irrelevant. What *is* important is the change in mental imagery.

To decide their verdicts, jurors placed Weinstein into a mental simulation of the alleged crimes. Well, what happens when they inject a visibly weak and feeble Weinstein into that simulation? Their mental picture becomes weaker and less vivid: *Is he guilty? Well, I'm having trouble picturing him committing those crimes. Maybe he is less guilty of the most egregious crime.*

Ultimately, Weinstein was, indeed, acquitted of the most egregious crime. Did the walker help? Perhaps. Or perhaps not. But the problem is that we'll never know for sure.

Mental imagery also influences your personal decisions, including life-or-death decisions. Each year, people die from hurricanes because they don't evacuate. You can blame that stubbornness on the lack of vividness in their mental imagery: *Hmm, should I evacuate?* [imagines the hurricane while the weather is still nice]. *I can't picture the hurricane coming. It probably won't be THAT bad. I guess I'll stay.*

This book will have many examples, but here's the takeaway for now: Every decision is dictated by the ease and vividness of a mental picture. Instead of ignoring this flaw in our brain, we need to acknowledge and understand it. If we understand motivation, the *true* motivation behind our decisions, we can make better decisions. We can save lives.

Just *imagine* how great that would be.

1

Vividness

WELCOME BACK.

If you skipped to this first chapter, you should read the earlier sections so that we're on the same page, so to speak.

By now, you understand the process behind decision making. You make every decision by imagining the outcome. If this imagery feels vivid and pleasant, you are more likely to make the decision.

Based on this notion, you can influence motivation in two ways:

1. Make good behaviors easy to imagine.
2. Make bad behaviors difficult to imagine.

This entire book will expand on these tenets. All of the future techniques might *seem* different, but they all originate from these two ideas.

In fact, you already encountered hidden examples in this book. Something devious was occurring in this excerpt from the opening pages:

> . . . if you are previewing this book, what are you hoping to find as you scan these words? What would trigger that moment of decisiveness where you suddenly say, "What the heck, I'll buy it."

What's sneaky about it? The last few words are instilling a mental picture in which you are buying this book. When these people eventually contemplate the real purchase, their brain will already possess a template for this event: *Hmm, do I want to buy this book? Well, I can picture myself buying it. Therefore, I must want to buy it because [insert a reason].*

You can spot this strategy in sales. Beginner salespeople emphasize rational reasons for buying. Expert salespeople emphasize rational *and* emotional reasons. The best salespeople, however, emphasize a third aspect: they get customers to imagine themselves buying or using a product. Many people overlook this strategy because it doesn't tell customers why should they buy it. Or what they'll gain from it. Or any rational reasons at all. Yet the mere presence of that imagery increases their likelihood of buying (Gregory, Cialdini, & Carpenter, 1982).

You can influence any decision by adjusting the clarity and vividness of this mental picture. Here are some ideas.

Describe Tasks in Concrete Language

As a broke college student, you wake up like any normal day—hungover from the night before. Eyes glazed over, you glance at your tasks for today:

- ▶ Study for chemistry midterm
- ▶ Talk to Professor Smith
- ▶ Ask mom and dad for money

Those tasks seem normal, right? But look closely—those tasks are painting blurry mental pictures because of the abstract wording.
The following tasks are identical, yet the new wording paints a more vivid mental picture:

- ▶ Review past exams in chemistry
- ▶ Send email to Professor Smith
- ▶ Call mom and dad (ask for money)

Let's highlight the detriments of the old tasks:

▶ **"Study for chemistry midterm."** You can "study" in different ways: reading a textbook, memorizing notecards, reviewing past exams, and more. This lack of specificity paints a blurry mental picture. You need a concrete task, like reviewing past exams, so that you can imagine this behavior: *Hmm, I can picture myself reviewing exams. This task should be easy.*

▶ **"Talk to Professor Smith."** What does "talk" mean? Email? Phone call? Office visit? Again, this multiplicity weakens your mental picture. You should describe this task with a clear image: "Send email to Professor Smith."

▶ **"Ask mom and dad for money."** Oh boy, this task is vague *and* embarrassing. If possible, avoid writing tasks that trigger negative emotions. Focus on the neutral behavior: "Call mom and dad." If you need to jog your memory for the negative aspect, use parentheses: "Call mom and dad (ask for money)." Interestingly, parentheses will weaken the intensity of this negative emotion.[2]

Put yourself in my shoes right now. This sentence didn't exist a few moments ago. In fact, this whole paragraph, this whole chapter, this whole book started as a blank canvas that could be filled with an infinite combination of words and sentences. Even now, as I type this sentence, there's a blank space in front of my cursor that keeps perpetually moving, and no matter how many words I type, trying to consume this empty space, I'm faced with a ceaseless uncertainty of the exact words to choose, and that's why—as you can probably tell by now—I'm merely stalling for time, distracting you with this obnoxious monologue, in hopes that I will eventually find the ending to this sentence. Ah, there it is. That feels better.

---

[2] See Chapter 18 on Literature in my book *The Tangled Mind*. I discuss ways that grammar, syntax, and other linguistic features influence the images that you create while reading.

Here's my point: Writing a book involves a lot of ambiguity. Imagine that you're an author, and you see this task on your calendar: "Write my novel."

Ugh, so vague.

You remain sitting at your desk, twiddling your thumbs, hoping that a jolt of motivation will suddenly appear. Spoiler alert: it doesn't.

You need to boost your motivation by transforming this vague task into something more tangible and concrete, something that you can easily imagine. Any undertaking, no matter how big or complex, will always contain smaller steps. This book was a culmination of five steps:

1. Download articles on motivation
2. Read articles and take notes
3. Categorize notes into an outline
4. Transform outline into written prose
5. Edit prose into a final version

Any of those tasks would be more motivating than a vague task to "write a novel." And, if those tasks still don't jolt your motivation, perhaps you need to make them *more* specific, as you'll see next.

Focus on the Smallest Next Step

On your calendar, you see one of the previous tasks:

▶ Transform outline into written prose

Unsure how to begin, you keep staring blankly at your calendar. You keep hoping that, if you stare hard enough, then maybe—*just maybe*—this task will disappear. Like David Copperfield himself.

Perhaps the problem lies in the remaining ambiguity: How *exactly* do you transform that outline? Which words should you choose?

Moments ago, I was experiencing that same feeling—this page was nothing more than a gargantuan wall of complex notes. My brain was a little peeved: "Nick, this is a mess. What am I supposed to do?" I felt paralyzed. I *wanted* to move. I *wanted* to write. But I was sitting there, motionless.

After dwelling on this painful irony, in which I was struggling to find motivation to write my book on motivation, I tried a radical idea . . . I applied the technique that I was writing about. I stopped focusing on the vague task of writing prose, and I started focusing on the next smallest step: deleting unnecessary information from my notes. Instantly the floodgates opened. Suddenly I possessed a clear mental picture: I could scan my notes and search for anything that seemed irrelevant or unnecessary (and remove it). Within seconds, I was traveling down this clear path.

Something else happened, too. While scanning and deleting notes, I felt a new burst of motivation. Ideas started flowing, and I could see myself not only deleting irrelevant notes but also writing full sentences with the notes that remained, an endeavor that seemed utterly impossible minutes ago. Turns out, I just needed to get started.

And recall this task from earlier:

▶ Review past exams in chemistry

Perhaps you're sitting at your desk, glaring at this task, feeling nauseous. Your brain wants to study, but your body keeps sitting there. Something is disconnected between your brain and behavior. So, how can you fix it?

You need to deconstruct this ambiguous task into a smaller first step. In other words, don't motivate yourself to review the exams; motivate yourself to place your exams on your desk. Your brain can easily imagine this task.

Once you accomplish this step, focus on the next smallest step: find the oldest exam. Did you find it? Okay, now look for the first incorrect answer. And keep repeating this process, transforming each next step into a clear mental picture.

After a few steps, you'll notice that this process is becoming unnecessary; you'll start feeling naturally motivated. Why? Because at this moment—right now—you are studying. Your recent steps have provided the necessary building blocks to construct a vivid mental picture of studying. You just needed these blocks. You just needed to get started.

Throughout our journey, if you ever need motivation to pick up this book, try focusing on the immediate next step. Don't focus on reading a chapter. Focus on *opening* this book. Once you open it, focus on reading a single paragraph. Or a single sentence. By that point, if you *still* don't want to read, then stop. At least now you'll make this decision without being influenced by the sneaky distortion of disfluency.

Identify the "When" of Behavior

Before calling mom and dad, you need to make another awkward phone call to your credit card company. Your payment is officially late. In hindsight, perhaps you didn't need that life-size portrait of Ronald McDonald after all.

You quickly dial the number before changing your mind, hoping that you reach a robot. A few rings later, you breathe a sigh of relief:

Hi, you've reached our automated call center . . .

Eventually, you hear these options:

▶ *If you are going to pay within 3 days, press 1*
▶ *If you can't pay within 3 days, press 2*

You press 1 . . . even if that means selling Ronald.
Next, you hear these options:

▶ *If you are going to pay within 24 hours, press 1*
▶ *If you are going to pay within 36 hours, press 2*

▶ *If you are going to pay within 48 hours, press 3*
▶ *If you are going to pay within 72 hours, press 4*

Huh? Is this step necessary? You already indicated that you would pay within 3 days. Why be nitpicky?

This extra step might seem unusual and slightly passive-aggressive. Yet, with a real company, this step influenced more people to pay their debt (Mazar, Mochon, & Ariely, 2018). Why? Because these instructions created a vivid mental picture. If people could pay at *any* time within 3 days, then their payment remained an abstract and intangible event with no foothold in reality . . . they didn't imagine themselves paying. However, specifying an exact time, like 48 hours, required a clear mental picture: *Hmm, if I'm paying within 48 hours, then I'll need to do it tomorrow when I get home from work.*

Similar results happened when researchers called 250,000+ households to remind them to vote. They influenced more people to vote by asking specific questions:

▶ What time are you voting?
▶ Where will you be coming from?
▶ What are you doing beforehand?

Those questions helped people imagine themselves voting, which boosted their motivation to vote.

When you need to perform a task, don't tell yourself: *I'll do it tomorrow.* Specify an exact time: *I'll do it tomorrow [after I eat breakfast].* The clarity of this mental picture will nudge you to follow through.

We're now reaching the end of this chapter, so you'll need to make the same decision from earlier: Should you continue reading? Or stop here?

If you stop here, don't leave with a vague notion to read this book at a "later" time. When *exactly* will you read again? Before bed tonight? During lunch tomorrow? After calling mom and dad? Create a vivid mental picture so that you and I can resume our journey.

SUMMARY OF VIVIDNESS

You judge the desirability of any decision by imagining the outcome. You can influence decisions by increasing the vividness of these mental pictures.

Mimic the Desired Outcome

Last week, a cashier at Target randomly gave me that $10 gift card. Strangely, I soon found myself contemplating whether I should sign up for the rewards card. Target was using a clever ploy. Until this moment, I had never pictured myself using their rewards card, but now—thanks to this gift card—I *could* imagine this behavior. My brain acquired the necessary building blocks to construct this mental picture.

Show the Real-World Usage

While browsing a furniture store, you evaluate products via mental pictures: *Would this table look good in my bedroom? Hmm, I can't picture it. It probably wouldn't.* Some furniture stores, like Ikea, overcome this problem by displaying example rooms that are decorated with their furniture. Now, customers *can* picture these items in their home. And they look great.

Show the Intended Behavior

Mental pictures could inform public policy. Political commercials might become unfairly persuasive if they animate or illustrate the actual voting behavior. Viewers will eventually reach the voting booth with this event—voting for Candidate B—already in their brain: *Hmm, I can see myself voting for Candidate B. Therefore, I want to do it.*

Display Photos in Your Calendar

Your brain translates writing into a mental picture. Why not skip the middleman? Instead of scribbling a message ("go to gym") in various spots on your calendar, you could attach a photo of yourself at the gym.

This photo is the imagery that your brain needs. Calendar apps could incorporate this feature, too.

Write Neatly

Messy writing degrades your mental pictures: *Hmm, something feels difficult. This task must be difficult.* The end result? Patients are less likely to take their medicine. Kids are less likely to do their chores. And coworkers are less likely to meet their deadlines. Always take the extra three seconds to write neatly.

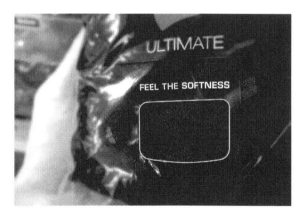

Communicate the Haptic Sensation

While buying socks, I noticed a package with a deliberate hole to let me feel the fabric, which is a clever ploy. Without this hole, I would have no idea how the socks feel. But now, I know *exactly* how they feel. I can imagine myself wearing them.

2

Ability

LOOK AT THE COVER of this book.

First, I chose the title—*Imagine Reading This Book*—to serve as a constant reminder of the key premise. Every time that you contemplate reading this book, the title forces you to construct a mental picture in which you are reading it: *Hmm, should I read this book? Well, I can picture myself reading it. Therefore, I want to read it.*

But there's something else in that cover, too. Do you see the hand that is flipping the bottom corner? This graphic illustrates the next principle: Your brain equates ability with desire. If a motor action is easier to do, you can imagine performing the behavior more easily: *Hmm, do I want to read this book? Well, I can see myself opening this book. So, yes.*

The key idea: You can boost motivation to perform a behavior by easing the *ability* to perform this behavior.

∞

Most objects have an "affordance" that allows you to interact (Gibson, 1979). Some doors have horizontal plates, in which you press the flat of your palm to push open. You can't pull because those plates don't "afford" the action of pulling. Some doors, however, have vertical bars that match the grip of your hand, so you intuitively grip to pull open.

You navigate the world by imagining yourself interacting with surrounding stimuli. Cups? You imagine grasping. Buttons? You imagine pushing. Puppies? You imagine squeezing. The more vivid these mental pictures, the stronger your motivation.[3]

For example, what would ease your ability to grab the following cup?

The cup already has a round shape, so we *can* grab it. Yet could we strengthen this affordance? Suppose that this cup was bending inward around the middle. Wouldn't this cup be easier to grab?

Indeed it would. While scanning the coffee aisle of a store, I noticed that store brands were using a regular cylinder for their container, whereas some popular brands were using an indented shape.

---

[3] Mental pictures don't need to be visual images. Even blind people can imagine themselves interacting with objects. "Simulation" is a more accurate term, but I'll stick with "mental picture" because this term . . . well . . . creates a stronger mental picture.

Immerse yourself into the mindset of a customer who is standing in a coffee aisle, debating which brand to choose, and suddenly noticing a container with an inward bend: *Hmm, I can see myself grabbing this coffee. I must want to buy it.*[4]

What else would ease your ability to grab the cup? Could we add or adjust something? Like a handle? Sure, that might help.

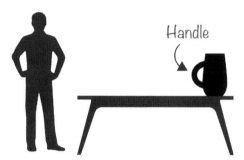

And, if we add a handle, we should consider its orientation. In one study, people were more likely to buy a cup when the handle was positioned toward the right (Elder & Krishna, 2012). Why? Because right-handed people—the majority of the population—could more easily imagine grabbing this handle. Left-handed people, needless to say, preferred handles pointing toward the left. Perhaps most interesting,

---

[4] Currently, researchers are perplexed why humans prefer round objects (see Bar & Neta, 2006). Some of them had believed that we simply dislike sharpness, but new evidence shows that humans also gravitate *toward* roundness. My guess? Since round objects are easier to grab, we can blame this preference on our mental pictures: *Hmm, I can see myself interacting with this round object. Therefore, I must prefer it.*

the effect disappeared for both groups when they held a tennis ball; with their hands occupied, nobody could imagine grabbing the cup.

Cups might seem irrelevant, but we can apply this mechanism with *any* decision.

Suppose that you see an "add to cart" button while shopping online:

Add to Cart

You will evaluate this decision by creating a mental picture: You will imagine clicking this button and adding the item to your cart.

Now, look closely at that sequence. Your mental picture—the key factor in your decision—was generated by the button. Therefore, any traits of the button, like fluency, will creep into your mental picture.

First, consider the text inside this button. In the previous chapter, we discussed how concrete words can strengthen your mental picture.

> **Weaker:** Talk to Professor Smith
> **Stronger:** Send Email to Professor Smith

Marketers can influence you to buy their products by choosing button text (e.g., "Buy on Amazon") that paints a clear mental picture of the behavior: *Hmm, do I want to buy this product? I can see myself buying it. So yes.*

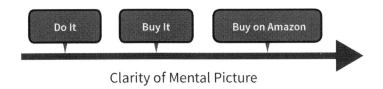

Clarity of Mental Picture

They can also make their buttons more clickable: *Hmm, I really want to click this button. Therefore, I must want to buy this product.*

What makes a button more clickable? How about color? Don't you need a visible area to click?

Indeed, during the 90s and early 2000s, industry data showed that people clicked buttons filled with color. However, in recent years, it seems like ghost buttons—buttons with an outside border, yet an empty inside—are becoming more common and effective.

[Buy on Amazon]   [Buy on Amazon]

I worked with a popular retail website with millions of visitors every month. They tested every variation of color for their primary button; and an empty button garnered the most clicks. Any guess why?

Here's my guess: New devices are changing the way our brains interact with computers. In the early days of the Internet, everybody used a mouse to interact. But today, thanks to the rising popularity of mobile and hands-free devices, many people are physically touching their screens.

Think about this interaction.

If you are interacting with your finger, then your brain is fixated on interactions that you can perform with your finger. Imagine that you see a solid button. How would it feel to press this button? Can you imagine the sensation? It's difficult, right? Every button in the sensory world has a different sensation—e.g., pressing a key on your keyboard feels vastly different than pressing an app on your phone. Despite these different sensations, you know *exactly* how it feels to push your finger inside an empty space because you would feel a sensory enclosure around your fingers. You *can* imagine this sensation.[5]

---

[5] Filled buttons are still effective in many contexts; ghost buttons require certain conditions (e.g., sufficient attention, finger interaction). I wanted to insert this disclaimer because many business folks are attached to the early studies with filled buttons. When I originally proposed this idea, a consultant in user experience, who coincidentally refers to himself as a UX comedian, wrote a scathing LinkedIn post about me, saying that I was a disgrace to the industry and that I should be ashamed of myself. Guess I really pushed his buttons (which I assume were filled).

Ghost buttons are one example, but hopefully you see the broader implication. Devices are changing the way that our brains interact with computers. With the advent of new devices on the horizon, these advances will be changing the psychological nature of our decision making. We need to understand these mechanisms in order to grasp the true impact of these technological changes on our perception and behavior.

Push Temptations Further Away

The clock turns 7:00 AM. *Beep. Beep. Beep.*

Your alarm is going off. You need to wake up, but you can't imagine leaving the bed. You hit snooze. Ten minutes later, you hit snooze again. And again. And you keep hitting snooze until reaching your daily epiphany that—*oh, right . . .* you have a job.

So, how can you stay awake? You need to weaken your ability to stay in bed. In a perfect world, you could program your bed to automatically tilt sideways, sliding you off so that you can't remain sleeping. But until the invention of that self-tilting bed, you still have a few options.

Next time, after hitting snooze, slide your alarm across the floor. A few minutes later, when your alarm goes off, you'll need to physically leave your bed to turn it off. By that point, you'll be standing (and your mental picture of staying awake will be more vivid). As a pro tip, you could also throw your covers onto the floor—without any covers on your bed, your mental picture of jumping back into bed will be weaker.

The key idea: Many people fixate on changing their *motivation* when they should be fixated on changing their *ability.*

Want to reduce your craving for junk food? You need to inhibit your *ability* to eat this food. Avoid bringing this food inside your home altogether, so that you will be forced to drive to the store to satisfy your craving. Any junk food that is readily available is junk food that you can imagine eating.

But what if your spouse or roommate needs a fully replenished stockpile of ice cream? You could still inhibit your ability in other ways. Google ran into this problem at their offices; they provide free snacks to employees—which is good for morale, yet bad for waistlines. Remarkably, though, a few minor tweaks reduced consumption by 3.1 million calories in seven weeks (Kang, 2013). Simple changes like:

- **Opaque Containers.** They placed candy inside opaque containers to block their visibility, and they placed healthy foods (e.g., granola, nuts, fruit) inside glass containers to make them more visible.
- **Eye Level.** They moved soda below eye level so that healthier drinks (e.g., water) were more visible.
- **Difficult to Reach.** They placed healthy food in front, making it more difficult to grab unhealthy food.

Once you control physical ability—or in this case, a lack thereof—your motivation will often follow. It's like placing a wall in front of the cup:

Bring Goals Physically Closer

You can do the opposite with *good* behaviors. You should make these behaviors *easier* to perform.

So, what else would nudge you to grab the cup? What if we pulled it closer? Wouldn't this proximity ease your ability to grab it?

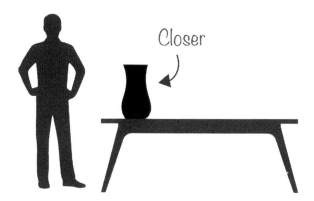

You bet. And again, this cup is merely symbolic of any goal. We could apply this proximity to anything.

Suppose that you want to eat more fruit, so you buy some apples . . . but, for whatever reason, you never eat them. Perhaps you're not eating them because you stuffed the apples inside a drawer of your refrigerator. Every time that you contemplate eating an apple, you need to imagine these steps:

> Stand up. Walk to fridge. Open fridge. Open drawer with apples. Open bag. Grab apple. Close bag. Close drawer. Close fridge. Walk to sink. Wash apple. Dry apple. Walk to couch. Eat apple.

I'm tired just reading that.

Instead of forcing your brain to imagine a gajllion steps to eat a single apple, you could keep a bowl of apples next to your couch (all pre-washed). Now, you only need to imagine two steps:

> Grab apple. Eat apple.

Your goal—eating fruit—is now closer. Your mental picture of eating an apple has become more vivid.

Need motivation to read this book? Don't place this book inside a bookshelf. Leave it on a table, tilted in your direction so that you can imagine grabbing and reading it. Eliminate all unnecessary steps before this goal.

You can even spot this effect with buttons. The designers of the iPhone positioned the payment window near the bottom of the screen because this location is closer to your fingers. You can imagine clicking this button more easily: *Hmm, I can see myself clicking this purchase button. I must want to buy this app.*

Other marketers add foreground cues. The makers of a popular app influenced more people to click a button by placing a horizontal bar behind it, which made the button seem closer to the user (and thus easier to click).

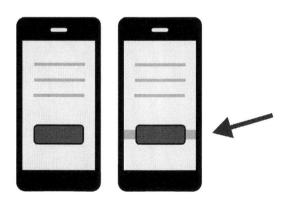

Recommend an Option

Congrats—you just secured a new job. Your new employer has a retirement plan, and you need to choose the amount that you want to contribute:

Yearly Contribution: $————

But *ugh*, this decision is vague. What number should it be? How high? Should you do it at all? You can't see a clear path forward, so you postpone the decision by saying, "I'll do it later."

Ten years later, you give it another go. But don't worry, your savings are only behind by . . . [checks calculator] . . . seven hundred thousand dollars.

Whoops.

It's amazing that one small tweak could have drastically changed your savings. Drastically changed your life.

So, what could have nudged you to make the original decision? The solution is simple: Whoever designs that question should recommend an option. I categorized this strategy into four stages:

▶ **Stage 1: No Recommendation.** Just a blank slot that needs to be filled with the yearly amount.

▶ **Stage 2: Offer a Suggestion.** Beneath the blank slot, there could be a statement that says, "Most people contribute 5% of their salary."

▶ **Stage 3: Fill a Placeholder.** The blank slot doesn't need to be empty. It can be filled with a placeholder number, like $2,000, that users could adjust.

▶ **Stage 4: Provide a Default.** The decision could be made for them. Perhaps, by default, the yearly contribution is $2,000, but employees can adjust this amount in the settings. Employees still control this decision, yet their savings aren't penalized by inaction. Some countries use these "opt-out" policies for organ donation (i.e., citizens are presumed to be donors unless they opt out), and this tweak dramatically boosts participation (Davidai, Gilovich, & Ross, 2012).

By Stage 4, the decision has already been made . . . we can't bring the goal any closer.

Place an Easy Task Before the Goal

You can also bring goals closer by manipulating the milestones before them. Suppose that you need to run 10 km. Which path seems easier?

- ▶ Run 2 km *then* 8 km.
- ▶ Run 8 km *then* 2 km.

Turns out, we prefer the difficult-to-easy path (i.e., 8 km *then* 2 km; Jin, Xu, & Zhang, 2015). This path, the researchers argued, seems easier because it tackles the difficult portion while our energy is highest.

And that could be true . . . but I see another culprit.

I suspect that we generate *multiple* simulations: We imagine the run from each milestone, and then we merge these pictures into an average. That sounds confusing, but I'll walk you through it.

Suppose that you need to run 8 km *then* 2 km.

You imagine running each section: You imagine running 8 km; then you imagine running the final 2 km.

Do you notice something? The 2 km section is very close to the final goal, isn't it? When you imagine running this final portion, you are reaching the 10 km goal very easily. And this mental picture feels good.

On the other hand, imagine running 2 km *then* 8 km:

This milestone is far away from the goal. When you imagine running the final portion, you still need to exert a lot of effort to reach the goal. In this setup, there is no mental picture in which you are easily reaching the final goal, so this run feels more difficult (and less desirable).[6]

Try placing a fun or easy task immediately before a goal. People will imagine the pursuit from this nearby milestone, and this final goal will seem easier to achieve. Does your business offer reward tiers? Narrow the distance between the top two tiers, which will make the highest reward seem easier to attain.

∞

Soon you will reach the end of this chapter. If you are reading the physical book, hopefully the final paragraph will end on the left-side page. Why? Because the next chapter will be visible on the right-side page. You'll be able to imagine reading this next chapter.

Some astute readers might be thinking: But Nick, either way, I'll

---

[6] Two caveats. First, an expert runner might prefer a difficult run. Always consider an individual's conclusion: *Hmm, this run feels difficult. I want a difficult run. Therefore, I'll choose it.* Second, even though we *prefer* a difficult-to-easy path (e.g., 8 km then 2 km), we're more likely to *accomplish* goals in an easy-to-difficult path (e.g., 2 km then 8 km). I'll explain why later.

be flipping the page to place my bookmark. I'll see the next chapter regardless.

That's a good point—but it still doesn't matter. You need to focus on the precise moment in which a decision is made. Compare these two decisions:

▶ **Ends on Left:** *Hmm, I can see the next chapter. I'll see how it is.*
▶ **Ends on Right:** *. . . and finished. Should I read the next chapter? Hmm, I can't see myself doing it. I'll stop here.* [turns page . . . places bookmark . . . closes book]

Affordances need to be visible *during* a decision; you need to feel the ease of this physical ability *while* you're making a decision.

SUMMARY OF ABILITY

You can boost motivation by easing the physical ability to perform a behavior. This heightened ability will ease the mental picture.

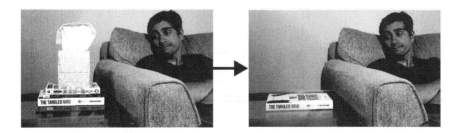

Ease the Ability to Perform Good Behaviors

Want to read more books? Don't keep multiple books under a tissue box. Keep a single book in an easy-to-reach spot, possibly oriented toward you.

☐ Basic Economy works for me

| Continue with Basic Economy | or | Economy for + $25/person |

Restrict the Ability to Perform Bad Behaviors

I stumbled upon this diabolical and frustrating interface while booking a flight. I was given two options: basic economy vs. upgraded economy. However, I could only click one option: upgraded economy. I needed to click a separate box to unlock the cheaper option on the left. This airline was restricting my ability to choose the cheaper seating.

Structure Decisions to Be Opt-Out

Maybe you were browsing Netflix last night when you noticed that they added *Fifty Shades of Grey*. You click to view the details, but you don't plan on watching it . . . you're classier than that. While you read the description, however, the movie starts playing automatically. A few seconds go by, and the details on screen slowly fade away. Before you know it, you're watching a movie that, moments ago, you fully planned to ignore. Netflix sucked you into this movie by easing your ability to watch; you no longer needed to click "play" or do anything at all. They made this decision for you.

Place "Good" Things Within Easy Reach

Inside your cabinet, move healthy foods toward your dominant side, and bring them to a lower shelf so that you don't need to reach far.

Guide Attention Toward the Motor Action

You are more likely to "swipe right" in a dating app when a candidate is looking toward the right (Van Kerckhove & Pandelaere, 2018). The gaze orients your attention toward that direction, easing your ability to swipe right.

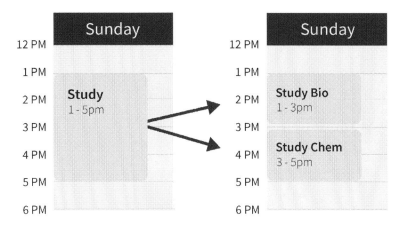

Separate a Large Task Into Smaller Units

A long 4-hr block to "study" can feel like a marathon. Dividing this task will make it seem easier (Redden, 2008).

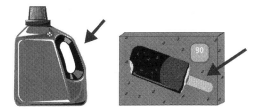

Orient the Affordance Toward the Right

Most people are right-handed. Place your affordance on the right so that most people can imagine grabbing these objects.

3

Body States

THE PREVIOUS CHAPTERS have been peeling the layers behind mental pictures:

Mental pictures need to be vivid.

This vividness is based on physical ability.

And now physical ability is based on . . . [pause for dramatic effect] . . . your body state.

Until now, we've been so preoccupied with the cup that we haven't addressed the person doing the grabbing. So, what about *you*? Could we tweak something about you to nudge your behavior?

Absolutely.

Mental pictures influence your decisions because you misattribute the vividness with a desire: *Hmm, I can see myself making this decision. Therefore, I want to make this decision.*

Your body plays a powerful role in this process:

▶ **Heartbeat.** When your heart is beating quickly, you find other people more attractive (Valins, 1966). *Hmm, my heart is racing. I must find this person attractive.*

▶ **Posture.** Blackjack players are more likely to "hit" on 16 while sitting upright (Huang et al., 2011). *Should I take an extra card? Hmm, I feel confident. So yes, hit me.*

▶ **Head Nodding.** While supposedly testing headphones by nodding their head, people agreed with the news broadcast that was playing (Wells & Petty, 1980). *Hmm, do I agree with this message? Well, I am nodding—so yes.*

Perhaps your body is influencing your opinion of this book: *Hmm, how do I feel about this book? Well, I'm highlighting a lot. So, I must be enjoying it.*

More relevant to this chapter, your body also influences the nature of your mental picture. Right now, imagine going to the grocery store.

Are you picturing it?

How does this picture feel? Easy? Difficult? If difficult, perhaps you could blame this difficulty on your current body state. Your brain is creating this mental picture by injecting your current body. Maybe you are . . .

. . . curled up in a blanket.

. . . sore from exercising.

. . . naked on the couch.

These traits are creeping into your mental picture, degrading your ability to imagine going to the grocery store (along with your motivation).

Here's another example.

Find an object far away from you, and imagine yourself moving to this distant landmark. What body traits would influence the ease or difficulty of this traversal? How about these traits:

▶ **Age.** Elderly people perceive hallways to be longer because they have trouble imagining the walk (Sugovic & Witt, 2013). *Hmm, it seems difficult to walk this distance. It must be farther.*

▶ **Weight.** Distant landmarks seem farther for people who are weighed down, such as heavy body weight (Sugovic, Turk, & Witt, 2013) or heavy backpacks (Bhalla & Proffitt, 1999).

▶ **Energy.** After people consume an energy drink, they perceive landmarks to be closer (Schnall, Zadra, & Proffitt, 2010). Sad music, thanks to its deactivation, makes landmarks seem farther away (Riener et al., 2011).

▶ **Tools.** Distant landmarks seem closer if you are sitting in a car because you imagine driving (vs. walking; Moeller, Zoppke, & Frings, 2016). Similarly, distant objects seem closer when a reaching tool is nearby (Witt, Proffitt, & Epstein, 2015).

▶ **Expertise.** Parkour experts estimate walls to be shorter because, unlike regular folks, they can imagine climbing those walls (Taylor & Witt, 2010).

Here's the key idea: Your brain constructs a mental picture by injecting your current body state. Want to boost your motivation to perform a behavior? Place yourself in a body state that will ease this mental picture.

The following sections will give you some practical ideas.

Activate a Helpful Body State

Do you *want* to exercise, but—for whatever reason—can't stir the motivation? If you are sitting down, feeling deenergized, then your mental picture of exercising will be weaker. Try these ideas:

▶ **Pace Across the Room.** Back-and-forth pacing will increase your heart rate, activating a body state in which you *can* imagine exercising.

▶ **Eat a Light Snack.** You could eat a banana and spoonful of peanut butter to boost your energy (and ability to imagine exercising).

▶ **Get Dressed.** Your pajamas, albeit comfortable, are degrading your mental picture of going to the gym. Change into workout clothes before you conclude that you're not motivated.

Whenever you are struggling to motivate yourself, activate a body state that resembles the intended outcome so that you can imagine this behavior more easily.

Alternatively, instead of adjusting your body, you could schedule tasks during a time of the day in which your body is naturally more capable of imagining these behaviors, as you'll see next.

Schedule Tasks During Peak Body States

Motivation ebbs and flows throughout each day, usually in a recurring pattern. But everybody is different: You might be motivated in the morning, whereas another person might be motivated in the afternoon.

Here's my recurring pattern:

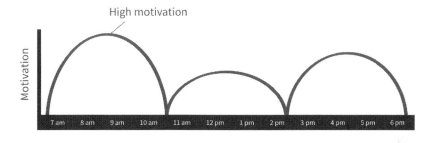

I'm highly motivated in the morning, but then it dwindles for a few hours around the early afternoon—which is when I exercise, shower, and eat lunch—and then it rises in the late afternoon (thanks to more coffee).

Many people, blinded by overconfidence, assume that they can control these waves. They plan their days by scheduling tasks at random intervals throughout each day because they believe, at any point, they can raise their motivation to perform these tasks.

Don't be one of those people.

It can be difficult to change your motivational waves. It's much easier to plan your day around existing waves.

Suppose that your motivation follows my recurring pattern—where it's high in the morning, low around noontime, and high in the afternoon. And suppose that you, too, are writing a book. You can make progress on your book in various ways, and these tasks require different levels of motivation. From most motivation to least motivation:

1. Write book
2. Read articles
3. Watch courses
4. Brainstorm ideas

One day, around 1:00 PM, you see the most difficult task "Write Book" at this time slot on your calendar. Unfortunately, 1:00 PM is also the recurring slump in your motivation. Your mental picture of this task will be weaker: *Hmm, I can't picture myself writing. Guess I'll scroll Instagram.*

You should have scheduled this difficult task for the morning, the peak of your motivational wave.

Always plan your schedule by striving to perform your *highest doable task (HDT)*. Your HDT is whichever task captures the largest portion of your motivational wave.

Your Highest Doable Tasks (HDTs)

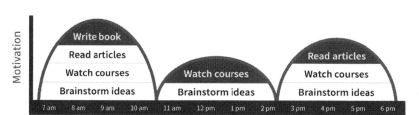

Perform the highest task that you can accomplish with your current level of motivation. Don't brainstorm ideas in the morning, the peak of your motivation, because you will be wasting idle motivation that you could have harnessed for a more strenuous task, like writing the book. High peaks of motivation are less common, so you should pounce on their availability by performing your highest doable task.

Also, if you can't stir motivation for one task, don't immediately conclude that you aren't motivated: *Hmm, I can't see myself writing the book. Guess I'm not motivated today. I'll scroll Instagram.*

You might not be motivated for this difficult task, but you *could* be motivated for a less strenuous task, like reading articles or watching courses. Always run a mental picture of the next lowest task in the ladder before giving up.

The takeaway: Your body experiences an ebb and flow of motivation throughout each day. Plan your days so that you are scheduling difficult tasks during the peaks of your motivation; these body states will ease your mental pictures of those behaviors.

Activate a Helpful Mindset

Which message would motivate somebody to exercise?

▶ The benefits of exercising (e.g., you feel energized)
▶ The detriments of *not* exercising (e.g., you feel sluggish)

It depends. Interestingly, people prefer the first message after receiving their paycheck from work. The further they move away from this paycheck, the more they start preferring the second message about preventing detriments (Mishra, Mishra, & Nayakankuppam, 2010). Try to solve this puzzle before the end of this chapter.

For now, let's revisit a childhood memory. Do you remember being the victim of this psychological trick:

Spell *top*.

Spell *hop*.

Spell *mop*.

Okay, what do you do at a green light?

Your brain is shouting "stop" because of the matching response, but that answer is incorrect.

You experience similar effects throughout each day. Suppose that you're loading a dishwasher:

Dirty cups? In.

Dirty plates? In.

Dirty utensils? In.

And now, you visit your computer to buy something on Amazon. Five seconds ago, you just repeatedly filled a container. And now you're filling a new container: your shopping cart. Could your earlier actions, much like the childhood trick, condition your response? Would you instinctively add more items into your shopping cart?

And what about similar actions with containers? Stuffing an envelope? Packing a suitcase? Filling a glass of water? Could those innocent behaviors condition your response in a subsequent context?

Let's see some evidence and examples.

1. Choosing Mindset

Which animal do you prefer: *elephant* or *hippo?*

In one study, this innocent question influenced people to buy a random product in a subsequent context. Why? Because most purchase decisions follow two stages:

> **Stage 1:** *Whether* to buy
> **Stage 2:** *Which* to buy

Choosing an animal instilled a *which-to-choose* mindset, placing people in that second stage where they assumed that they already decided *whether* to buy.

Imagine that you just toured a gym, and the manager asked you to complete a survey with multiple-choice questions.

Goals? You choose cardio.

Amount of exercise? You choose once per week.

Rate the tour? You choose 8.

Then *bam* . . . you see two options for membership: 6-months or 1-year. Your repetitive choices have just activated a burning compulsion to choose one of these membership options, instilling an implicit assumption: *Hmm, I want to choose a membership. Therefore, I want to buy a membership.*

2. Hiding Mindset

Many actions, such as filling a dishwasher or filling a shopping cart, share a deeper behavior (filling a container).

Emotions have deep behaviors, too. Suppose that you feel embarrassed. What's your deeper urge? You want to hide from the world, right? In that case, which products could help you hide? Maybe sunglasses? Sure enough, when people reflected on a real-life embarrassment, they were more likely to buy sunglasses (Dong, Huang, & Wyer, 2013).

Imagine that somebody is contemplating whether to become a member at the previous gym. Brand new to the fitness world, this person feels embarrassed with his current body (especially compared to the beastly figures in the gym). When the manager asks him to sign up, perhaps his decision—yes or no—will be influenced by his current location. If asked in the main lobby, next to a barrage of windows, and in view of other members, he might feel an uncertain sensation: *Hmm, something doesn't feel right. I'll get back to you.*

However, if asked in a closed office, an office that is shielding him from the external world, perhaps this enclosure would match his deeper urge to deflect attention: *Hmm, this decision feels right. I'll sign up for a year.*

3. Attention Mindset

What's the deeper urge of jealousy? It's the opposite: You want somebody to notice you. Well, what products help you get noticed? Maybe bright clothing? Like a bright coat? Interestingly, that's what happens: Jealous people were more likely to buy a brightly saturated coat (Huang, Dong, & Wyer, 2017). This coat was fulfilling a deeper need to capture attention.

4. Attacking Mindset

Arguments rarely have a winner. No matter what you say, or how strong your argument is, your opponent is fixated on attacking whatever comes out of your mouth. In order to get your message heard, *genuinely* heard, you need to start with something that your opponent can't attack. You need to start with points of agreement.

Want your boss to increase your budget? You might be tempted to start your presentation with strong arguments. But be patient, my friend. Start with slides that emphasize a shared agreement: "We both want to: achieve our projections, stay under budget, appease the higher-ups." Your boss will be forced to adopt a mindset of agreement, which will pry open their mindset to future points in your presentation.

As a backup plan, you could try acknowledging their attacking behavior. If you tell them that it feels like they are instinctively attacking your arguments, then—paradoxically—the only way to attack this argument is to refrain from further attacks.

5. Acquisition Mindset

Have you ever made the mistake of shopping for food while hungry? In this body state, you can imagine eating everything on the shelves.

And, strangely, hunger strengthens your desire for *all* products, even products that are inedible (Xu, Schwarz, & Wyer, 2015). In one study, people were more likely to purchase binder clips when they felt hungry, even though we don't eat binder clips. And hey, no judgment if you do.

But what caused this desire?

Think about the deeper behavior: Your hungry brain is attuned to pulling something (i.e., food) closer, and it extends this desire to other stimuli: *Hmm, I really want to pull these binder clips closer. Therefore, I must desire them.*

Consider eating something before you go shopping. Otherwise, you might feel a craving for every product that you see.

Oh, and did you solve the mystery from earlier? Why do people prefer the benefits of exercising (e.g., more energy) after receiving a paycheck? Why aren't they persuaded by the detriments of not exercising?

Your recent paycheck increased your purchasing power, enabling you to acquire objects via purchasing. Your brain is pulling things closer. You prefer messages that emphasize benefits (e.g., more energy) because you pull these benefits closer. Other messages (e.g., avoid sluggishness) involve pushing something away, which is incongruent with this mindset.

∞

Soon you will reach the end of this chapter, and you will face the same recurring decision: Do you stop here? Or continue?

I threw a lot of information at you during this chapter, so your brain might be feeling tired or drained. And that's problematic: *Hmm, I can't see myself reading the next chapter. I'll stop here.*

So, do me a favor: Blink your eyes and vigorously shake your body. Do this even in public . . . just tell bystanders that the man inside the book told you to do it. They'll understand.

Alright, feel better?

Taking a few seconds to breathe and blink can jumpstart your mental capacity, placing you in a body state that can imagine continuing.[7]

---

[7] Then again, perhaps blinking would backfire. Jean Mandler, a researcher in child development, recounted a time when another researcher—Jean Piaget—failed to get his 9-month old daughter to blink. Piaget kept blinking, but his daughter kept opening and closing her hands. But wait . . . blinking involves closing your eyes, right? And she was closing her hands? Are we seeing a deep behavior? To quote Mandler: "his children were expressing a concept of opening and closing. They had the right idea but couldn't locate the right part. The concept was abstract: opening and closing per se . . . a more abstract representation of the act itself" (Mandler, 2004, p. 32). Would repeated blinking activate a mindset of closure? Would these blinks condition you to close this book? It's plausible. To be safe, don't blink for the rest of the book.

SUMMARY OF BODY STATES

You create mental pictures by injecting your current body. You can boost motivation by placing yourself in a body state that eases these mental pictures.

Get Dressed Before Cancelling

You scheduled a first date for tonight, a date that you were initially excited about—but now that it's here . . . not so much anymore. Perhaps you can blame your lack of enthusiasm on your pajamas. Your brain might be injecting this version of yourself into the date: *Hmm, something feels awkward. I don't want to put myself through this.* Your mental picture will become more vivid (and desirable) if you change into real clothes. Always get dressed before canceling.

Stokkete/Shutterstock.com

Don't Shop While Tired

Participants in one study memorized a number—either a 7-digit number or 2-digit number. Turns out, the 7-digit number influenced people to choose cake over salad (Shiv & Fedorikhin, 1999). Preoccupied with the long number, they gravitated toward the option that ignited the strongest emotions. Avoid shopping when you feel tired; otherwise, you might be vulnerable to the emotional pull of unhealthy options.

Advertise Haptic Products on Mobile

You've heard the saying: *When you're a hammer, everything looks like a nail.* Here's a new saying: *When you are interacting with your finger, everything looks touchable.* While shopping on your mobile device, you prefer tangible products because you can imagine touching them. In one study, mobile users preferred a sweatshirt over a city tour (Brasel & Gips, 2014). In another study, they preferred furniture over Wi-Fi (Brasel & Gips, 2015). If your product has a strong haptic sensation, consider shifting more advertising dollars into mobile.

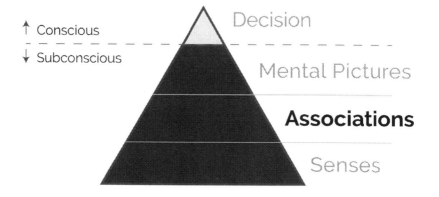

STAGE 2

Associations

DOWN WE GO, deeper into the brain.

Where do mental pictures come from? Let's jump inside our microscopic ship and travel to the source: neural associations.

Consider the concept of *toothpaste*. How did you learn this concept? Well, you needed to attach this idea to something that already existed in your brain, like *teeth* and *cleaning*.

Thanks to this learning process—i.e., attaching new concepts to exiting concepts—your knowledge has become an interconnected web, in which toothpaste is connected to many related ideas. Some connections are strong (e.g., floss, mouthwash, Colgate). Some connections are weak (e.g., shampoo, deodorant, bathroom).

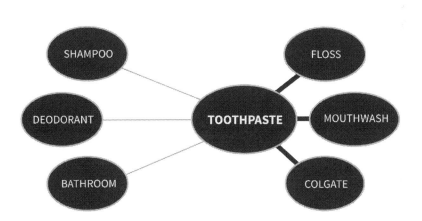

It's a simple idea: All concepts are interconnected in your brain. The stronger the relation, the stronger the connection.

Now, you also experience *spreading activation*, in which activating one concept disperses a wave of activation toward adjoining concepts. For example, as you read this section, the concept of toothpaste is being activated in your brain, dispersing activation toward the concepts that are connected to it. Stronger connections are receiving more activation.

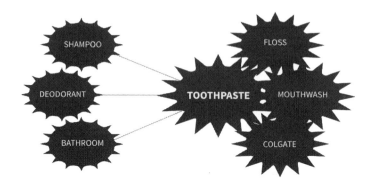

Activating concepts in your brain will activate any concepts that are related. Stronger relationship? Stronger activation.

Here's an illustration. Think of a lucky dwarf. Got it? Okay, now think of a number between 1 and 10.

In many instances, a "lucky dwarf" will influence you to think of 7. Why? Because the number 7 is related to luck (e.g., lucky number seven) and dwarves (e.g., *Snow White and the Seven Dwarves*). By thinking of a lucky dwarf, you activate the concepts of *luck* and *dwarves,* which disperse activation toward 7 on a nonconscious level. You tend to choose this number because it pops into your mind more easily.

You saw a similar effect earlier in this book. You were more likely to buy Captain Morgan after watching a strange commercial with 31 repetitions of "Captain." This commercial activated Captain Morgan on a nonconscious level, so you were more likely to choose it.

What else can activate concepts? Turns out, a lot.

Next time that you walk into a retail store, pay attention to the subtle cues around you, like the background music. French music nudges you to buy French wine, while German music nudges you to buy German wine (North & Hargreaves, 1999). Each nationality is activated from the music: *Hmm, something about this French wine feels right. I must want to buy it because [it'll taste better].*

Or consider these pizza deals:

- ▶ 4 small pizzas with unlimited toppings for $24
- ▶ 4 small pizzas with 6 toppings for $24

Economically, the first option is superior because it offers unlimited toppings. Yet, in one study, people were more likely to buy the second deal with 6 toppings (King & Janiszewski, 2011).

Look at the second deal. Does something feel unusual about it? Say, oddly familiar? As if something feels right?

Hmm, 4 and 6? Aren't they multiples of 24? Indeed, they are. Upon seeing that $24 price, people felt a weird sensation because this number was already activated in their brain: *Hmm, something about this deal feels right. I must want to buy it.*

Some final examples of activation:

▶ **Colors.** Perhaps the red handle of your shopping cart would influence you to buy strawberries over blueberries.[8] This red handle activates the concept of red, so your mental picture of buying strawberries—a red fruit—will be stronger. It sounds crazy, but this effect happened with pen colors. While circling products in a survey, people chose green products if they were using a green pen, yet they chose orange products if they were using an orange pen (Berger & Fitzsimons, 2008). *Hmm, something about this green product feels right. I must want to choose it.*

▶ **News Events.** In 1997, media outlets were covering the news story of NASA landing on Mars. Coincidentally, or perhaps not, the makers of Mars Bars noticed a weird spike in sales near this time (see Berger, 2016).

▶ **Previous Ads.** After seeing an ad for mayonnaise, people were more likely to buy any condiment, like ketchup (Lee & Labroo, 2004). Mayonnaise activated the overall idea of condiments and—by extension—ketchup.

The following chapters will disentangle the concept of spreading activation, uncovering some peculiar effects that influence your perception and behavior in everyday life.

---

[8] See my YouTube video—The Psychology of Choice—for other examples.

4

Activation

ON THE PREVIOUS PAGE, the final sentence hinted at some peculiar effects of activation that "influence your perception and behavior."

That very phrase contained a peculiar effect: Each outcome—perception *and* behavior—seemed less important because of a quirky flaw with spreading activation.

Let's illustrate this idea with a goal. For example, think of one reason why you should save money. Maybe student loans? Your brain will attach this reason to your goal:

In this setup, your goal—saving money—is dispersing *all* of its activation toward student loans. This reason is becoming highly activated.

But now, consider three reasons for saving money: student loans, retirement, and vacation. Turns out, spreading activation is a zero-sum mechanism. Your brain will be distributing a finite amount of activation among these multiple reasons:

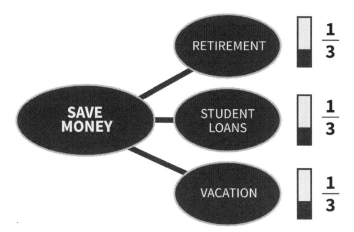

Even though you possess multiple reasons to save money, you ironically become *less* likely to save money. Indeed, residents of rural India were less likely to save money when researchers emphasized multiple reasons (e.g., college, retirement, health care; Soman & Zhao, 2011). They were more likely to save money with a single reason (e.g., college).

Or consider the opposite side. Instead of reflecting on *reasons* to save money, think of three *ways* to save money. Perhaps these:

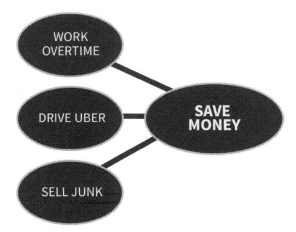

Activation, yet again, is traveling down multiple pathways in the reverse direction—each idea is becoming less activated. In one study, multiple ways to lose weight (e.g., jogging, kickboxing, eating less) seemed less effective than a single way (e.g., jogging; Bélanger et al., 2015).

Don't worry if you feel lost or overwhelmed. The key strategy involves consolidating activation into a single behavior so that you create a stronger mental picture of this behavior. The following sections will teach you easy ways to apply this principle.

Emphasize a Single Way to Reach a Goal

This chapter argues that you're more likely to reach a goal when you focus on a single way to get there.

But first, here's a caveat.

Show Multiple Ways Before the Pursuit

Remember the cup? Suppose that you are staring at this cup with multiple reaching tools nearby.

With so many tools available, reaching for this cup should seem incredibly easy.

However, upon reaching, you discover something: This goal is tougher than you thought. Your brain becomes inundated with questions. Which tools are available? Which tool is best? Should you use the Reach-o-Matic 2.0? Or the Reach Deluxe 2000?

Multiple tools *seem* appealing, but—in reality—a single tool would have been more effective. This clear path would have narrowed your focus toward the goal, eliminating any superfluous decisions (e.g., which tool to use).

So, here's the caveat: Although you're more likely to reach a goal when you focus on a single way to get there, you mistakenly prefer multiple ways to accomplish this goal.

Before you pursue a goal, focus on the multiplicity of options. If a patient discovers an illness, doctors could explain multiple remedies and treatments; this multiplicity would make the goal (e.g., getting better) seem easier to achieve. From here, doctors could then motivate their behavior by funneling their attention toward a single remedy or treatment.

Still with me? There's one more thing.

A single path is more effective, right? So, why do we prefer multiple routes? Why don't we see the benefit of a single pathway?

In early stages of goal pursuit, your brain is focused on "how" to get there. Remember our three ways to save money? Before the pursuit, your brain is focused on those three nodes:

Those nodes are sending multiple waves of activation toward the single goal of saving money; this goal is becoming highly activated. However, once you start pursuing this goal, you reverse the directionality: Activation starts traveling from this single goal toward multiple pathways, becoming diluted. Multiple nodes are helpful *before* the pursuit, but they are detrimental *after* the pursuit.

Okay, take a breather. I threw a lot of information at you. The remainder of this chapter will focus on practical applications.

Allocate 100% Focus Toward a Means

You're sitting on the couch, waiting for a burst of motivation to push you to the gym. Then . . . *ding*. Lightbulb moment. You could bring the audio version of this book. That way, you can work out *and* listen. You'll kill two birds.

Thirty minutes later, you step onto a treadmill, as you listen to the narrator speak this very sentence. And perhaps you feel a bit strange, hearing the narrator speak a sentence that is directly mentioning him. It's like breaking a fourth wall. What is the narrator thinking while speaking this sentence? Or this sentence? Must feel weird for him. Or perhaps the narrator is too focused on the narration; perhaps he doesn't realize that you and I are discussing him right now. Could he interject to answer these questions? Would the publisher remove his comments?

Before you know it, your train of thinking has completely derailed. While your mind has been racing about the narrator, your body has been walking at an embarrassingly slow pace. You snap your focus back to exercising, and you increase the speed on the treadmill.

But *ugh*, a few minutes later, you feel exhausted. You try to endure a bit longer, but for some reason, you just don't feel motivated. You press stop, drive home, and return to the couch for another bowl of ice cream.

We've all been there.

So, why did you lose motivation? If you analyze that scenario, you'll notice that your goal—going to the gym—was activating two reasons: exercise *and* listening to this audiobook.

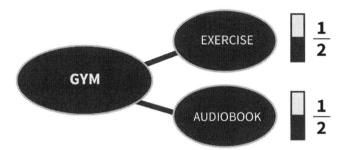

Each reason became diluted. You became less motivated to exercise because the audiobook was stealing activation from this reason for going to the gym.[9]

Resist the temptation to kill two birds with one stone. If you are at the gym, then focus on the gym. Don't listen to an audiobook. Don't brainstorm ideas for your business. Don't call your friend. Allocate one hundred percent focus toward exercising so that you create a vivid mental picture of this behavior.

Want to read more books? Don't leave multiple books on your coffee table; this multiplicity will dilute the activation. Leave a single book so that your brain can imagine reading this specific book.

Analyze your life to find situations in which you are diluting activation among multiple options. Struggling to find that special someone? Perhaps you are dating multiple people simultaneously and diluting the activation among them: *Hmm, do I want to commit to this person? Well, I can't picture myself with this person. Guess I'll keep searching.* You might have better luck with an isolated approach in which you date one person until making a decision.

Or how about your late-night booty call? If one person in your life is fulfilling multiple roles—friendship *and* physical pleasure—then perhaps those roles are becoming diluted. Both outcomes might be less gratifying.

---

[9] Would music cause this effect? Generally, no. Most people use music to *enhance* the goal of working out (e.g., it pumps them up). This mindset sends *more* activation, rather than diluting it.

Same with parents who befriend their children. Those two roles—parent *and* friend—aren't additive; they don't merge into a superhuman form of parenting. You become less of a parent. And less of a friend.

Weaken the Activation of Irrelevant Goals

In addition to *strengthening* a desired behavior, you can also *weaken* irrelevant behaviors—which will consolidate more activation toward the intended behavior.

Here are some ideas.

Block Leftover Options

You just grabbed a chocolate from an assorted box, but you see the remaining chocolates staring at you. Your chosen chocolate will taste better if you cover the box with a lid (Gu, Botti, & Faro, 2013). You will now be focusing more attention on the chosen chocolate, preventing those peripheral options from diluting your enjoyment.

After choosing an option, block your view of the remaining options:

- ▶ **Choose a Meal?** Close the menu.
- ▶ **Choose a Vacation?** Toss the competing brochures.
- ▶ **Choose a Relationship?** Delete any dating apps.

Your fear of commitment can be counterproductive. Sometimes you seek backup options in case your current choice doesn't pan out, yet the mere presence of these alternative options can dilute your enjoyment, sabotaging your commitment in the first place. So, get rid of them.

Invest Minimal Time on Backup Plans

Likewise, sometimes you can't help but entertain the worst-case scenario: *What if I fail? What am I going to do?*

You might hear that inner voice next time you deliver a speech: *What if I can't remember my talking points?* You start worrying. Which makes you worry more. Soon you find yourself worrying about worrying. Trapped in this vicious cycle, you decide to write your speaking notes, in hopes that this backup plan will salvage your speech if things go downhill.

Unfortunately, studies confirm that this backup plan will hinder your success (Napolitano & Freund, 2017).

The more time and resources that you spend on a backup plan, the more you divert activation away from the main goal. A greater investment in Plan B will decrease the likelihood of Plan A succeeding.[10]

Deemphasize Irrelevant Reasons

While speaking to a friend, you mention that you might study in Chicago because it has a lot of good schools. Your friend says, "Ah, that's great. My buddy studied in Chicago. He has family there."

Whoops. Your friend's innocent remark just made you less likely to study in Chicago. Can you spot the reason?

Before this conversation, your reason—Chicago has good schools—was the main reason behind your decision, so it was receiving *all* of the activation. But now, your friend mentioned a new reason for studying in Chicago: family. And you *don't* have family in Chicago.

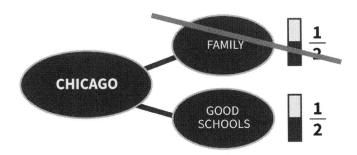

---

[10] Obviously, use your judgment. Don't quit school to become a professional unicycle repairman because this book told you to chase your dreams.

This new reason—family—steals activation from your other reason, and then it vanishes. Gone. *Poof.* And it takes the stolen activation with it. You now possess a weakened version of your original reason (see Zhang, Fishbach, & Krugalinski, 2007).

Many websites make this mistake by mentioning *all* of the reasons for buying a product. Suppose that you sell an eye tracking device, in which the applications—business, gaming, health care—are very different from each other. Your website should isolate these visitors onto pages that are only relevant to them. Perhaps you could ask them to select their field:

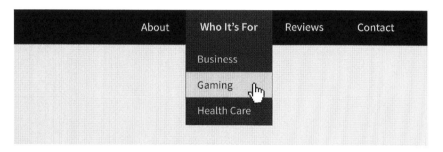

This function will bring them to an isolated page where you can communicate the benefits that are most relevant to their needs. You won't be diluting this information with irrelevant benefits from other domains.

Reduce the Aesthetics of Undesired Options

You might have heard about the *beauty bias,* in which beautiful people seem more sociable, intelligent, and many other positive traits. This bias exists because we misattribute the visual aesthetics of somebody's appearance: *Hmm, something about this person feels good. Therefore, this person must be [smarter].*

The same effect happens in graphic design. Beautiful websites are persuasive because we misattribute the aesthetics: *Hmm, this website feels good. Therefore . . .*

   . . . *this news article must be accurate.*

. . . this service must be valuable.

. . . I must want to buy something.

Even sneakier, the reverse can happen. Suppose that you see a purchase button, along with a "No Thanks" option underneath. Clever marketers could nudge you to click the purchase button by enhancing its aesthetics, but the *really* clever marketers could simultaneously nudge you away from the "No Thanks" option by *reducing* its aesthetics, perhaps by shifting this text slightly to the left:

If this imbalance were so subtle that you didn't notice it, then you'd feel a weird sensation about this "No Thanks" option, as if something didn't feel right. This uncertainty could nudge you toward the buy option: *Hmm, something about this "No Thanks" option doesn't feel right. I must want to choose the buy option.*[11]

Weaken the Activation of Rewards

On a Sunday afternoon, you are well-prepared.

Cookies? Check.

Netflix? Check.

Cow-print pajamas? Check.

All prepared for a mind-blowing experience, you press play on the new crime docuseries. But something happens. Perhaps your guilt was

---

[11] Marketers could also adjust the text: "No Thanks" is a polite response that many users can imagine saying. However, a blunt "No" is so direct that many people will have trouble imagining this response. Likewise, some marketers add exclamation points (Buy Now!), but this inflated excitement is harder to imagine.

catching up with you. Or perhaps it was the infamous "buh-duhhh" sound on Netflix that jolted you awake. You quickly turn off the TV and, for the next 10 minutes, you battle with yourself:

"Get to work."

"No"

"You need to."

"No"

"This is your last weekend to get work done."

"No"

You keep eyeing your laptop, but no matter how badly you want to walk over and start working, something is holding you back.

As a final attempt, you negotiate with yourself: "Okay, if I work for 2 hours, *then* I can watch Netflix. Deal?"

"Deal," says your brain. And you finally get to work . . . not realizing that this internal negotiation, albeit effective in the short-term, harmed your long-term success.

∞

Rewards are usually the first weapon to combat low motivation. Think of most institutions: jobs reward you with salaries, schools reward you with grades, volunteering rewards you with warm, fuzzy feelings.

Yet, in recent decades, researchers have discovered that rewards can sometimes *reduce* motivation. Rewards can strip you of autonomy, as if your actions are being controlled by an external force, and this finding is casting doubt on widespread functions in society, like salaries and grades. Are those rewards harmful? Are jobs and schools, the pivotal institutions in society, structured in the wrong way?

And it gets more complicated. Despite evidence *against* rewards, many researchers are producing evidence consistent with the original assumption that rewards *are* motivating (see Deci, Koestner, & Ryan, 1999 for a review).

So, what's going on? Are rewards motivating?

The short answer: Yes.

The long answer: It's a little more nuanced.

This section will clarify those discrepancies. By the end of this section, you'll know why some rewards can be harmful, and you'll know how to structure rewards so that they *are* motivating.

∞

Did you know that carrots can help you read?

I lied, they can't. Well, maybe they can—I'm no carrot expert. But I wrote that statement to illustrate a point: You now believe that carrots are less tasty (Maimaran & Fishbach, 2014).

Ten seconds ago, you perceived two main reasons for eating carrots: healthy and tasty.

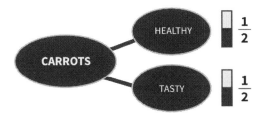

First of all, notice the dilution? You tend to assume that healthy foods are less tasty. Or that tasty foods are less healthy. Part of this perception can be blamed on spreading activation.

Second, and more relevant, your brain—after discovering that carrots could help you read—attached a third node:

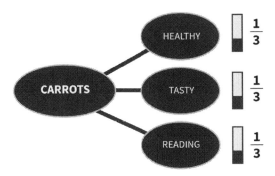

This third reason was siphoning activation away from the "tasty" node, so you perceived carrots to be less tasty.

Rewards can be detrimental because they produce a similar effect. One main reason for performing *any* behavior is enjoyment. Rewards are problematic because they attach a new reason to this behavior, siphoning activation away from your enjoyment:

This behavior is now less enjoyable because of the mere presence of the reward.

Fortunately, you can prevent this harmful effect by applying the following techniques.

Reduce the Saliency of Rewards

When possible, reduce the saliency of a reward so that you preserve your enjoyment. Each time that you reward yourself for trudging through a task, you are telling your brain that this behavior requires trudging.

Remember the Netflix reward?

I can watch Netflix if I work for 2 hours.

This reward is problematic because you are *only* working to receive this reward. The *more* you activate this reward, the *less* you activate enjoyment.

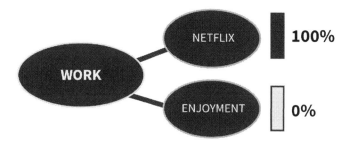

Activation is finite. If you are only working so that you can watch Netflix, then you *aren't* working because you enjoy this behavior.

A few hours ago, I experienced this effect. As a latecomer on the Game of Thrones bandwagon, I was anxious to binge the series after work today. The problem? It was only 3 PM . . . I still needed to write for a couple hours.

Ugh.

I had been enjoying writing, but once I fixated on this reward, everything changed. Now I kept looking at the clock every few seconds:

"3:00 PM . . . 3:03 PM . . . 3:04 PM."

I felt agony. Writing became less enjoyable because my brain had shifted the activation from enjoyment to reward. I was no longer working because I enjoy writing; I was working so that I could receive the reward.

Luckily, I overcame that hurdle by thwarting my ability to watch Game of Thrones: I moved away from my home office, which is next to my living room TV, and I situated myself on the outside balcony, orienting my body away from the living room. And it worked. Otherwise, I would have *further* thwarted my ability by driving to a coffee shop.

Are you struggling on a run? Don't motivate yourself by focusing on an external reward, like the dessert that you can eat later. Focus on the intrinsic pleasure of running so that you preserve your enjoyment.

Reduce the Saliency of External Pressure

Pushy salespeople often backfire: If customers feel like they *need* to perform a behavior, then they no longer *want* to perform this behavior.

My book title—*Imagine Reading This Book*—could backfire for some readers who perceive this title as an attempt to influence their behavior. This extrinsic pressure could siphon activation from their intrinsic desire.

Reduce the Saliency of Metric Output

Resist the urge to measure the sheer output of behavior, such as buying a pedometer to count your walking steps. You will no longer be walking for enjoyment; you will be walking to increase the numerical output on this screen. And you will be less motivated (Etkin, 2016).

While reading this book, don't focus on the sheer number of pages that you read. Focus on the experience of reading.

Make Rewards Contingent on Performance

Many researchers disagree over rewards, but the vast majority agree on the following: You shouldn't reward people for participation.

For example, teachers could offer gold stars based on participation or performance:

> **Participation:** Gold stars for *doing* problems.
> **Performance:** Gold stars for *solving* problems.

Performance rewards, albeit subtle in distinction, are vastly more effective because they sever the connection between the reward and behavior. These rewards are no longer telling students: "This task is so boring that I'm giving you a star to endure it."

Instead, this reward is now . . . a reward. A bonus. A congratulatory symbol of an accomplishment. It's telling students: "You deserve a star because you performed this behavior well."

Some students might feel cheated if they don't receive a star, yet their peers receive one. But there are loopholes to overcome this detriment.

For example, let's solve the infamous quandary with participation trophies. Can you give *every* child a trophy? Even if their team lost? Sure, you can—*but you need to specify a reason.* Give the winning team a trophy for winning. Give another team a trophy for sportsmanship. Give another team a trophy for best cheering. Give something unique to every team: highest attendance, most improved, best defense, *anything.* These trophies won't be rewarding children for simply *doing* the behavior, so the intrinsic reasons, like enjoyment, will remain.

The takeaway: Don't reward people for simply *doing* a behavior. Specify a contingency so that any reward becomes a congratulatory symbol, leaving enjoyment as the main reason for this behavior.

SUMMARY OF ACTIVATION

Activating a behavior in your brain will help you imagine this behavior. However, activation is zero-sum: Multiple nodes will dilute the activation. Therefore, consolidate activation by strengthening a single behavior or weakening irrelevant behaviors. And pay careful attention to rewards, which can dilute your enjoyment.

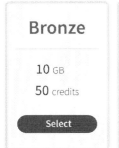

Increase the Saliency of a Desired Option

Clever marketers can nudge you toward an option by visually distinguishing it—e.g., background color, the words "most popular" above it, arrows pointing to it, or anything else. This option becomes more activated (and thus desirable). Sometimes customers will choose this option without simulating the other options. They might have felt positive emotions from the adjacent options, too—perhaps even *stronger* emotions—but they fail to notice these emotions because they stop simulating.

Mark Various Options

You should distinguish options even without a desired option that you want people to choose. Amazon marks some options with "Bestseller" or "Amazon Choice" because these markers increase the activation of these options, strengthening your desire to buy them.

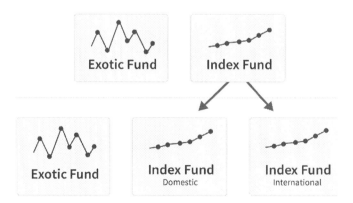

Split Favorable Options Into Multiple Units

People tend to distribute resources evenly across options. With two investment funds, safe and risky, they will invest money into the risky fund. You could reduce this behavior by splitting the safer fund into two accounts. Now, when people distribute their money, the mere presence of two safer funds will siphon a larger portion of their money (Benartzi & Thaler, 2001).

Aim Variety Packs Toward Beginners

Fitness beginners are more likely to buy protein bars in a variety pack with different flavors (Etkin & Ratner, 2012). If you are just beginning a goal, like fitness, your brain wants to see multiple ways to reach it. The multiplicity of a variety pack makes the fitness goal seem easier to achieve (and thus more appealing).

5

———

Habits

EXHAUSTED FROM a stressful day at work, you arrive home with one thing on your mind. One thing that can make you feel better. One thing that can numb the pain.

Ice cream.

You open the cabinet to grab a bowl. With arm in mid-air, fingers nearly clutching a bowl, you experience a moment of hesitation. Your inner voice starts questioning this behavior: "What am I doing? Do I *really* need this?" After a brief pause, you agree. You return the bowl and close the cabinet.

Indeed, you grab the full container of ice cream and head toward the couch . . . a bowl seemed foolishly unnecessary.

Collapsing on the couch, you start drowning your sorrows with spoonfuls of cookie dough. Each bite so sweet, so delicious, so comforting—you feel the pain melting in tandem with the ice cream.

Halfway down the container, your brain checks in: "Hey, it's me. You've eaten quite a bit. Maybe we should stop here."

Yet your arm, like a rogue agent, rebelliously scoops deeper . . . and deeper . . . and deeper. One moment you're staring at a full container of ice cream; the next moment you're frantically scraping the sides and bottom for any microscopic traces that could be lingering.

Then you wait for the next phase of this episode. You've been down this road before . . . you know what's coming.

A few minutes later, right on schedule, you start feeling an emotional mixture of regret, shame, and stomach pain. You start hating this decision. You start hating yourself.

Amidst this horrible feeling, you tell yourself that you won't do it again. You recite this statement every time, and . . . here you are . . . yet again . . . saying it for the 15th time. But no, this time you really— *really*—mean it.

Moving forward, how can we stop this behavior? And how can we build good habits, such as eating healthy and exercising? Most important of all, how can we do those things without feeling restrained or inconvenienced? How can we enjoy these seemingly mundane behaviors?

This chapter will answer those questions.

∞

You are more likely to perform a behavior if you activate this node in your brain. And, as you learned in the previous chapter, you can activate this behavior by activating concepts that are connected to it.

But how do these concepts become connected in the first place? You can blame *co-occurrences*: If two concepts frequently appear together in space or time, they become connected in your brain.

Think about recurring habits in your life, such as eating ice cream after a stressful day at work. If you frequently pair these behaviors, then your brain is binding these two nodes: (1) stressful day at work, and (2) eating ice cream. Eventually, the cue—stressful day at work—will immediately trigger this behavior because of the connection.

Researchers illustrated these ramifications in a series of experiments. In a preliminary study, people indicated that "taste" was the main reason why they ate popcorn while watching movies. So, imagine if those people received 7-day old stale popcorn that was unappetizingly bland. They should eat less popcorn, right?

In theory? Yes.

In reality? No.

At Duke University, researchers recruited students to watch movie trailers, and nearly everyone opted for free popcorn. The researchers, however, sneakily altered the freshness: Some bags were popped 1 hour ago, whereas other bags were popped 7 days ago. Intuitively, people should have eaten less stale popcorn. But what happened? People who frequently snacked on popcorn ate the same amount they usually did, regardless of staleness (Neal et al., 2009). They weren't eating because of the taste; they were eating because of the habit.

The researchers ran another study with similar results: If people attended many sports games on campus, then—upon seeing a picture of a stadium—those people started speaking louder without realizing it.

In both studies, a specific cue (e.g., movie theater, sports stadium) triggered a behavior that frequently occurred with this cue (e.g., eating popcorn, talking loudly).

Today, all of your habits—good *and* bad—are immediate, knee-jerk reactions that formed over time. These behaviors are merely activated by a cue in your environment. In this chapter, you'll learn how to apply this knowledge to stop bad habits and create good habits.

Detach Cues From Bad Habits

To break any bad habit, you need to find the cues that are activating these responses. For example, eating ice cream could be triggered from six cues:

1. **Emotion**—*I've had a rough day. Feed me ice cream.*
2. **Time**—*Oh look, it's 8:00 pm. Time for ice cream.*
3. **Location**—*I'm at the mall, and I usually get ice cream.*
4. **People**—*Zach likes to meet at the ice cream shop.*
5. **Action**—*After dinner, I like to eat something sweet.*
6. **Object**—*Oh look, ice cream in my freezer. Let's eat it.*

Those cues trigger your behavior of eating ice cream. To break this habit, you either need to remove those cues or replace the behavior.

Option 1: Remove the Cue

Let's switch gears to examine another bad habit: distraction.

Like any Monday morning, you arrive to work with a sadistic number of unread emails and leftover tasks. You start prioritizing the coworkers who will be least angry when your work arrives late. But then:

Buzz.

"Hmm, a vibration? On my phone? I wonder what it could be."

Then, *whoosh*—in an instant, you get sucked down a rabbit hole of mindlessly scrolling social media. Expense report? Who has time? You need to check what your high school friend's brother's cousin ate for lunch today.

An hour later, like someone waking up from hypnosis, you feel a jolting mixture of regret and confusion: "What have I been doing?"

As you ponder this question for another thirty minutes, you start realizing that today might be slower than usual . . . even though this distraction happens every Monday. And Tuesday. And Wednesday.

So, how can you break this habit? The first step involves finding the original cue that triggered this distraction . . . the *buzz.*

Much like Pavlov's dogs who salivated upon the ring of a bell, we instinctively grab our phones upon feeling that buzz. If you remove that buzz, then you remove that knee-jerk reaction to grab the phone. Perhaps:

- ▶ **Silence Your Phone.** No buzz? No distraction. Unless, of course, you check the time. Then you'll get sucked in. So:
- ▶ **Wear a Watch.** I suspect that, since the early 2000s, humans have been checking the time more often. Why? Because we get rewarded for it. In today's world, checking the time is often rewarded with a mindless distraction. Consider wearing a watch so that you don't need to look at your phone.
- ▶ **Leave Your Phone Elsewhere.** Every morning, you could keep your phone in another room, a locked drawer, or anywhere else besides your immediate grasp.

Now, what about ice cream? We could remove *some* cues from the six categories: we can go to a different mall or we can rid our lives of Zach. But for the most part, those cues are difficult to remove.

If we can't remove a cue, then we need to replace this behavior. For this step, we can borrow a strategy from Indiana Jones.

Option 2: Replace the Behavior

In a classic movie, Indiana Jones swapped a valuable object with a decoy object. You can follow the same strategy with your bad habits.

Many people attempt to break habits by stopping the behavior altogether—e.g., they stop eating ice cream. But this strategy is like stealing a valuable object without replacing it. Your brain is expecting a particular response, and it will notice the absence of a response. Like Indiana Jones, you need a replacement behavior that will trick your brain into believing that everything is the same. Nothing has changed.

But how? You can't replace ice cream with kale. That's like Indiana Jones replacing the small idol with a Ford Fiesta. Something won't seem right.

Instead, move gradually: Start with a behavior that feels similar to the old response. This approach is similar to a phobia treatment, known as *systematic desensitization,* in which you gradually expose people to increasingly fearful stimuli.

Afraid of spiders? First, you'd talk about spiders—that's not too bad. Then, you'd see . . .

. . . pictures of spiders.

. . . fake toy spiders.

. . . spiders in virtual reality.

. . . real spiders in the distance.

. . . real spiders in a cage.

. . . real spiders without a cage.

Those baby steps desensitize your fear, until you no longer experience the crushing anxiety with real spiders.

You can follow the same strategy to break habits. Suppose that you eat ice cream every night after dinner, but you want to eat healthier. You need to replace this behavior with a response that feels similar—perhaps you could eat frozen yogurt. Frozen yogurt is basically like ice cream, except a little healthier. And sure, frozen yogurt is no kale . . . but healthiness isn't the goal right now. Frozen yogurt is accomplishing an important step of rewiring your brain: It's detaching the connection between dinner and ice cream, and it's reattaching this connection to frozen yogurt. This new foundation will help you build an even healthier response later.

After eating frozen yogurt for a few weeks, you can take another baby step: You can replace frozen yogurt with regular yogurt. Your brain would have rejected regular yogurt in the beginning because this response is very different from ice cream. But now, things have changed: Regular yogurt *is* connected to frozen yogurt. Any desire for frozen yogurt will be activating regular yogurt, too—this option has become more acceptable to your brain.

And now look at you . . . a regular Indiana Jones, swapping one behavior for a different behavior. If you wanted, you could stop here because regular yogurt is healthier than ice cream. Or you could take more steps, perhaps switching to a healthier yogurt, like Greek yogurt. Then a few weeks later, maybe Greek yogurt with kale. Before you know it, you replaced ice cream with a healthier food. All without any painful restraint or willpower.

You can follow this strategy for *any* habit. Do you sometimes lash out in anger, perhaps slamming or punching things?[12] You could try diverting this force toward an appropriate outlet, like a punching bag. This similar response could satisfy your old habit, while providing an intermediary step to build a better habit. Eventually, you could replace this punching bag with vigorous exercise—a similar, yet healthier solution. You could stop here, or you could take more baby steps, perhaps replacing vigorous exercise with Tai Chi.

---

[12] Most important of all, seek professional help to resolve any deep-rooted issues that might be fueling your anger in the first place.

It's tempting to break habits with a cold turkey approach, an abrupt and full cessation of the harmful behavior. It *seems* plausible, even admirable, but this approach is destined to fail. If you jump from ice cream to kale, then you will trigger negative emotions with this new behavior. Every time that you perform this behavior in the future, you will activate those negative emotions, making it harder and harder to endure this habit, until you eventually throw in the towel.

There is no reason to follow that path when you can stop bad habits without any pain. Without any sacrifice. Without any effort. You just need to make small, imperceptible adjustments to the behavior. This strategy is vastly more effective because it avoids those negative emotions, while keeping the positive emotions from your old habit.

To recap, you can break a bad habit in two ways: You can either remove the cue (e.g., don't keep ice cream at home) or you can gradually replace the behavior (e.g., replace ice cream with frozen yogurt and then regular yogurt).

In this past section, we used an existing habit to build a better habit. In the next section, you'll learn how to build a good habit with a blank slate.

Attach Good Habits Incrementally

Your best friend won't shut up about meditation. A few weeks later, you're convinced. You set a goal to meditate for 30 minutes each day.

Fast forward through time, and you'll likely see this pattern:

> **Day 1:** You meditate for 30 minutes.
> **Day 2:** You meditate for 30 minutes.
> **Day 3:** *I'm busy. I'll do it tomorrow.*
> **Day 4:** You meditate for 10 minutes.
> **Day 5:** *I'm busy. It's a weird week . . . it'll change.*
> **Day 6:** *I'll meditate eventually.*
> **Day 7:** *Eh, do I need to meditate? I'm fine without it.*

This pattern happens all the time with different habits: You are committed in the beginning, yet your motivation quickly plummets, until you convince yourself that you don't want to pursue the goal anymore.

Why does that pattern occur? And how can you stay committed? You can follow three steps (adapted from Fogg, 2019).

Step 1: Find a Cue
Step 2: Attach Incremental Behaviors
Step 3: Celebrate the Behavior

Step 1: Find a Cue

Charles Duhigg, journalist and author of *The Power of Habit*, describes how Febreze nearly failed in the beginning. The marketing team had originally positioned Febreze as a spray that could remove nasty odors from clothes and fabrics. They took an existing cue—nasty odor—and attached Febreze as the habitual response, in hopes that people would use Febreze every time that they smelled something funky.

The problem?

People become desensitized to smells. Very few people were smelling a nasty odor that would prompt them to buy and use Febreze. There was no cue. And thus, no habit.

On the brink of failure, the marketing team made a last-ditch effort: Instead of positioning Febreze as an odor-remover, they repositioned it as an air freshener to be sprayed at the end of cleaning, as a way to disperse a pleasant aroma. This new cue—the end of a cleaning routine—was a more salient and noticeable cue, which prompted people to use Febreze. This simple tweak ignited sales and catapulted the brand into enormous success.

To establish your own habit, you need to find a noticeable and recurring cue that will trigger your desired behavior. The most prominent technique is called an *implementation intention*, which resembles an IF-THEN approach: *When I see [cue], I will do [behavior].*

- ▶ **Flossing:** When I put my toothbrush back, I will floss.
- ▶ **Nutrition:** When I pour my coffee, I will take a vitamin.
- ▶ **Relationships:** When I get home from work, I will kiss my spouse.

If you can't find a recurring cue, then create an artificial cue by tying a red string in various places:

- ▶ **Fridge Handle:** When I see the string, I will grab healthy food.
- ▶ **Nightstand:** When I see the string, I will read a book.
- ▶ **Trash Can:** When I see the string, I will recycle.

Those cues are important for two reasons. First, it's not enough to be motivated; you also need to *remember* your goals. Sure, you can vow to stop overindulging on ice cream . . . but this promise is useless if it slips your mind a few days later. An external cue, like red string, provides a tangible reminder of your commitment, at the exact moment you need it.

Second, you unleash the power of spreading activation. Frequent pairings build stronger connections in your brain. Every time that you brush and *then* floss, your brain will strengthen this connection. Over time, flossing will become more activated and desirable.[13]

Some additional tips:

- ▶ **Choose a Logical Fit.** I used to hate going to the gym, but I genu-inely enjoy it today. So, what happened? I found a logical cue. Each morning, I begin the workday by reading academic papers, which I love . . . but even a nerd like me will become drained in

---

[13] There's a difference between desire and enjoyment. I've been flossing my teeth every night for the 30 years I've been alive. And maybe longer if I was able to find floss in the womb. But do I enjoy flossing? Not really—it's tedious and boring. Yet do I feel a burning desire to floss every night? Absolutely. Would I feel weird and anguished if I don't floss? Definitely. I don't enjoy flossing, but I desire this behavior.

a few hours. By late morning, my brain *needs* a break. Anything. At this moment, I can easily imagine going to the gym.

▶ **Avoid Specific Times.** You might be tempted to set timely goals, like exercising at 11 AM. But your schedule will inevitably change: meetings will change, coworkers will be chatty, new fires will need putting out. If your meeting ends at 11:15 AM, then *whoops . . .* your brain acquired an excuse to skip exercising that day. Choose recurring cues that are independent of time (e.g., pouring coffee, showering, putting on shoes).

▶ **Look for Waiting Periods.** Each day is filled with waiting: waiting for the shower to get hot, waiting for water to boil, waiting in the elevator, waiting for computers to start. Take advantage of these dull moments by inserting smaller habits. Perhaps you could focus on a positive sentiment while walking into work: *After I shut my car door, I will think of one thing I'm excited for that day.*

Once you find a cue, you can start attaching the incremental habit.

Step 2: Attach Incremental Behaviors

Much like bad habits, good habits need to avoid any drastic changes that feel grueling or demanding. If you currently run 0 kilometers each day, then you might feel tempted to run 5 kilometers each day. But slow down, my friend. You are making a drastic lifestyle change that requires a lot of strength and willpower, arduous emotions that you don't want to infuse with your new habit. Again, any emotions that you feel during this habit will become infused with the behavior.

Earlier we replaced bad habits by gradually adjusting the *type* of behavior (e.g., ice cream to frozen yogurt). To build good habits, we can adjust the *quantity* of behavior.

Want to meditate for 30 minutes each weekday? First, you need to find a recurring cue, perhaps: taking off your shoes when you get home from work. This cue will remind you to meditate.

As a go-getter, you might be tempted to pursue this goal with full force. If your current regimen is 0 minutes of meditation each day, then I agree . . . it's *tempting* to make up for lost ground with a lofty goal, like 30 minutes. But fight this temptation. You need to avoid negative emotions—inconvenience, effort, annoyance—that will enter your new habit. Future meditations will activate these emotions.

Start with a quantity of meditation that doesn't feel taxing. If you won't feel pained with 30 minutes, then sure . . . perhaps it's fine. But if you feel annoyed, then reduce that quantity until you reach a number that feels easy and doable. Maybe 5 minutes. Maybe 30 seconds.

But Nick, a 30-second meditation? How would that help me?

It might not. Right now, your goal isn't to meditate; your goal is to establish the habit. This meditation, albeit short, will be adjusting the neural wiring in your brain. Within a week or two, you will send a burst of activation toward meditation immediately after taking off your shoes; this meditation will be easier and more desirable.

Pretty soon, you will realize that you can meditate for a longer duration, maybe 10 minutes, without a backlash of negative emotions. From here, you can start raising that quantity to higher levels until reaching a desired goal, like 30 minutes. Good habits, much like bad habits, can be established through small adjustments to your daily routine.

True motivation shouldn't be difficult. If you find yourself needing willpower to trudge through a task, then something is wrong. Most people follow this path of resistance . . . and that's why most people fail a few days later. Creating a habit is much easier and more effective with incremental adjustments that connect a recurring cue with a small behavior.

And, finally, the last step involves solidifying this new behavior with a positive emotion.

Step 3: Celebrate the Behavior

Every time that you contemplate a new habit, like meditation, you should feel good about it. Luckily, these positive emotions often arise naturally. When people sprayed Febreze at the end of their cleaning routine, a moment in which they felt relieved and happy, they infused this positive emotion with Febreze.

Hopefully your meditation will feel naturally rewarding, as an opportunity to destress from work. If not, then be proactive: celebrate with a pat on the back, metaphorical or literal. Take a moment to recognize and appreciate your achievement, no matter how small or insignificant it seems. This celebration will inject a positive emotion into your new behavior, establishing a sturdy foundation on which to solidify this new habit.

SUMMARY OF HABITS

Your habits—good and bad—are triggered by recurring cues in your life. You can stop bad habits by removing these cues or gradually replacing the behavior. You can build good habits by attaching small amounts of this behavior to a recurring cue.

| Eat Food | Eat With Friend | Hang With Friend |

Gradually Replace a Behavior

Want to stop grabbing food whenever you feel bored? Start eating with a friend. Your brain will associate boredom with this new social behavior, and eventually the mere act of socializing can become the new solution to boredom.

Leave Remnants of the Old Habit

For the past few weeks, I would normally watch TV after the workday. But recently, I wanted to watch a few online courses. The problem? This mental picture didn't feel good; my brain wanted to watch TV because of the habit. Fortunately, I found a loophole by leaving the TV running in the background with zero volume. The mere presence of this background image fulfilled the need in my brain: *Finished work? Now TV? All set.* Suddenly I *could* imagine watching courses because I was fulfilling the old habit.

Remind Yourself of the Promise

Did you make a promise to stop a behavior? Tie a string to this temptation so that you remind yourself of this promise whenever you reach for this temptation in the future.

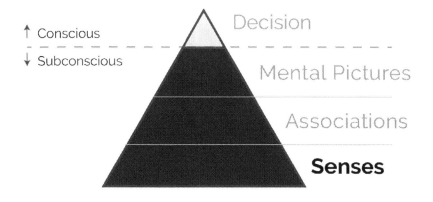

STAGE 3

—

Senses

IT WAS 2012.

I found myself sitting at a table surrounded by marketing professors, all of whom were giving me a strange look.

It was an academic conference, and my undergraduate paper was accepted. I hadn't realized that this acceptance was unusual until I was looking around the banquet hall, noticing that I was the only undergraduate among hundreds of marketing professors.

Undeterred, I turn to the person toward my left and begin with a simple, "So, where are you from?"

Visibly annoyed, he retorts with, "Where am I *from*? Or where do I *live*? Those are two different things."

Yikes . . . okay.

I turn to the person toward my right. She had just received an award, so I was nervous to speak with her because I assumed that she was a prestigious researcher. And me? I was just a nobody undergraduate.

We chatted for a bit, and I told her that I was interested in subconscious factors that influence behavior. Instantly her genuine smile transformed into a forced smile.

Her words said: "Oh . . . that's great."

Her eyes said: "Oh . . . so you are at this conference by mistake?"

Eventually, she described her stance by saying, "I don't research subconscious factors because you can't measure them." She said it with a tone implying that *nobody* should research them.

I've had similar experiences with other academics. Mention the term "subconscious," and you can be treated like a conspiracy theorist who claimed that the moon is made of cheese. I was even hesitant to use the term "subconscious" in this book; most researchers prefer the euphemistic term of "nonconscious."

But we should remove this stigma. Subconscious factors aren't pseudoscience; there are principles beyond our conscious awareness that profoundly influence our perception and behavior, fueling important decisions not only in our personal lives but also in society. We can't ignore these principles. We need to research and understand them.

In the following chapters, I'll describe these deeper elements of mental pictures. Your images contain hidden features that guide your decisions, all without your conscious awareness.

∞

As we discussed, you learn new concepts by attaching them to existing concepts—which leads to an interesting question: If everything in your brain is attached to an earlier concept, what if we retrace these connections? As I pose in my book *The Tangled Mind*:

> In order to learn Concept Z, you attached the meaning to an earlier concept, like Concept Y. Well, how did you learn Concept Y? You did the same thing: you attached Concept Y to an earlier concept, perhaps Concept X . . . Like an endless string of knowledge, what if we keep pulling? Wouldn't we eventually find a starting point? And, if so, what would it be? Wouldn't those concepts be infused into everything that we know today? (Kolenda, 2019, pg. 2).

Indeed, your web of knowledge had a starting point. A small handful of primitive concepts fueled everything that you know today, from capitalism to bromance. So, what *are* those primitive concepts? What fueled your entire knowledge? The short answer: *sensory concepts*.

You entered this world without knowing anything, except the confusing mixture of sensory concepts surrounding you. Every new idea that you learned was built onto this sensory foundation. Today, everything that you know has been constructed from sensory building blocks.

Consider your concept of time. Right now, imagine what you'll be doing next week. Got it? This mental picture, an image that you constructed in milliseconds, is profoundly mysterious.

For one, time is abstract. You can't see it. Or feel it. Or interact with it in any way. So, how did your brain create this mental picture? What were you picturing? And how did your brain know that this image was different from, say, tomorrow? Or next year?

When you deconstruct the concept of time, you find sensory concepts lurking underneath. You can spot these concepts by analyzing language, which is filled with spatial metaphors of time:

> Let's not spend a **LONG** time discussing this idea. I want to keep **MOVING** through this book so that we can finish in the **NEAR** future.

Whaddaya know . . . time isn't so abstract after all. When you envision time, your brain isn't using voodoo magic to construct an image from nothing; your brain is using sensory concepts—length, motion, distance—to provide a tangible skeleton for this otherwise intangible concept.

Your brain learned abstract concepts, like time, by attaching these ideas to sensory concepts. And this neural structure leads to an interesting effect: Anything that impacts sensory concepts will impact the abstract concepts that contain them.

Imagine that you see a tree in the far distance. How does it look? Probably blurry and hazy, right? You can't see the clear details.

Okay, now picture an event in the distant future: Think of what you'll be doing in five years. Are you thinking?

This event was "far" away from you in time. Since your brain used spatial distance to construct this image, you triggered the previous effect: This image seemed blurry and hazy. Researchers investigated this idea by asking people to color a blank drawing of a housewarming party. When the party was occurring in a few days, people filled this drawing with many colors; however, when the party was occurring in five years—the distant future—they filled this drawing with more variations of gray because their mental picture was hazy, as if this event were appearing in the far spatial distance (Lee et al., 2017).

Any spatial effect will be inherited by time. For example, cities seem spatially closer when they are displayed in simple fonts (e.g., Boston vs. *Boston*). Naturally, time would inherit this effect: Future dates will seem closer when they are displayed in simple fonts (e.g., January 15 vs. *January 15*).[14]

This idea will make more sense in the ensuing chapters. You will soon discover that sensory concepts, like spatial distance, breathe life into many abstract concepts, like goals. Remember the cup from earlier?

We've seen various strategies—bringing it closer, easing our ability, priming a body state—but those strategies are insufficient. We still need something else to reach this cup.

We need motion.

---

[14] Or consider date formats: the easy format of January 15, 2030 would seem closer than 01/15/2030.

6

Motion

WHICH DAY FEELS closer: yesterday or tomorrow?

Both days are equidistant from the present moment, yet most people perceive tomorrow—the future—to be closer (Caruso, Van Boven, Chin, & Ward, 2013). I'll explain why in a few paragraphs.

For now, let's discuss motion. From the moment you ventured into this world, moving objects have surrounded you. It's everywhere. This sensory concept is so primitive and pervasive that it became a frequent building block that helped you learn many future concepts, injecting these future concepts with the physical laws of motion.

Consider the law of momentum. When people watched a moving box suddenly vanish on screen, they consistently guessed that it disappeared further ahead because of the momentum:

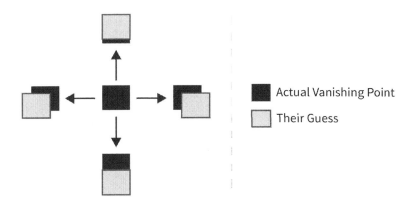

■ Actual Vanishing Point
☐ Their Guess

(Most guesses were also lower because of momentum *and* gravity.)

Sensory momentum creeps into many aspects of your daily life. You experience momentum with your own body: While reaching the midpoint of a subway ride, you feel closer to the destination because you displace your forward momentum (see Maglio & Polman, 2014).

Even more interesting, this effect can illuminate the earlier mystery with time. Why does the future feel closer than the past? Because your concept of time is built with motion: your brain imagines yourself *moving* toward the future. Therefore, the future feels closer because you are displacing your forward momentum.

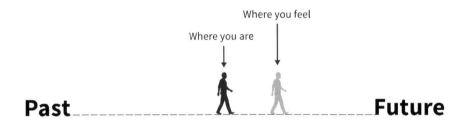

Motion is a key building block in *many* concepts, injecting these ideas with momentum. You believe that . . .

. . . if stocks are rising, they will keep rising.

. . . if your team is catching up, you will win the game.

. . . if you are winning at roulette, you will keep winning.

These mental pictures are built with motion from the sensory world, so these images inherit the physical laws of motion (e.g., momentum).

Goals are built with motion, too. Any goal—losing weight, starting a business, earning a degree—is conceptualized as a point in the distance, a spatial gap that you need to traverse with motion. Consequently, this mental picture inherits the physical laws of motion. If you understand the laws of motion, then you can depict your goal in a way that seems easier and more desirable. This chapter will give you practical techniques.

Experience an Early Win

Newton's first law of motion is *inertia*: An object at rest stays at rest. In other words, sensory motion is most difficult in early stages.

Intriguingly, you hear similar phrases while pursuing a goal: "The hardest part is getting started." And that's no coincidence. Starting a goal feels difficult because you haven't moved yet. Your body is at rest.

In order to jolt your motivation, you need to provide your brain with a sense of motion so that you overcome this inertia. How? You need to achieve some progress toward your goal; any progress will push you along this path, giving you momentum to continue. Your pursuit will become easier because, according to your brain, you will be in motion . . . and objects in motion stay in motion.

Here are some ideas.

Endow Progress in the Beginning

Always start with progress above zero. For example, at a car wash, researchers distributed two loyalty cards: Version A required eight stamps, whereas Version B required ten stamps (with two stamps already in place).

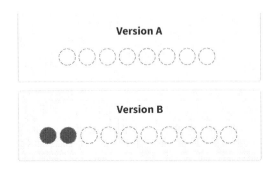

Both cards required eight stamps, yet Version B nearly doubled the redemption rate (Nunes & Drèze, 2006). Those two stamps endowed people with progress. The remaining stamps felt easier because of the inherent motion: It felt like rolling a ball that was already moving.

Remember our cup? Endowed progress would resemble an outstretched hand:

Even within this new graphic, can't you imagine this person grabbing the cup more easily? Any indication of motion (e.g., outstretched hand) helps your brain simulate the continued progression.

You can also apply this trick near the end of a workday. It's tempting to end a workday after finishing a task, such as writing the final paragraphs of a chapter. But tomorrow, you'll be starting a new task from scratch. No motion. No momentum. Therefore, before finishing the workday, strive for *some* progress on your next task; perhaps you could write a few sentences in the next chapter. When you resume this task tomorrow, you will already possess motion. I call it the *finish-after-starting effect.*[15]

Determine the task that you will do tomorrow morning, and then make progress on it:

▶ **Cleaning Your House?** Lay out the supplies.
▶ **Filing Your Taxes?** Organize the paperwork.
▶ **Sending an Email?** Draft the outline.

This initial motion, much like an outstretched hand, will help you imagine the continued progression.

Arrange Goals From Easy to Difficult

Remember these tasks:

▶ Review past exams in chemistry
▶ Send email to Professor Smith
▶ Call mom and dad (ask for money)

You will be more likely to complete those tasks if you arrange them from easy to difficult (Jin, Xu, & Zhang, 2015). Perhaps you could send the email, then review exams, then call mom and dad. Easy tasks give you momentum to accomplish difficult tasks.

You could also:

▶ **Show Tangible Progress Quickly.** Fitness trainers should help new clients lose weight in the easiest (and fastest) way possible, even if this outcome doesn't represent true weight loss (e.g., water weight). Any progress feels like motion, which helps people harness the full extent of their motivation.
▶ **Aim For Low Hanging Fruit.** Launching a new product? Need

---

[15] Or, if desired, the *FART effect.*

feedback from potential customers? Start with people you can easily access, like friends and family.

▶ **Postpone Obstacles to Later Stages.** I noticed that the 30-min TV program, ABC World News Tonight, schedules more commercials in the second half. The first half is devoid of them, whereas the second half is filled with many commercials. I'm only speculating, but I suspect that this scheduling retains more viewers. The first half builds momentum, which helps viewers endure commercials in the second half. Well played, ABC World News.

Start With Broad Goals . . . Then Specific Goals

Motion can clarify a frequent misconception with goals. Take a guess. Which goal is more motivating?

▶ Lose 10 lbs.
▶ Lose as much weight as possible

Most self-help experts recommend the first goal; if you listen closely, you can hear them shouting, "Goals should be specific."

But is that *really* true? Not always, according to our brain. The reason involves how we conceptualize progress.

Imagine that you set a goal to lose 10 lbs. After trips to the gym, you manage to lose 1 lb. Is that good or bad? It depends. You'll answer that question by comparing 1 lb. to the reference point—in this case, 10 lbs. Hmm . . . doesn't seem great, does it? Your progress of 1 lb. is far from the goal of 10 lbs.; and this slow progress will demotivate you.

On the other hand, imagine that you set a goal to lose as much weight as possible. What's the reference point? It's a beginning marker of 0 lbs. Aha, now the comparison—0 lbs. vs. 1 lb.—seems more drastic and motivating. Abstract goals can be equally (if not more) motivating than specific goals.

However, let's see this scenario play out. Suppose that you keep exercising, and you lose a total of 8 lbs. Suddenly things have reversed: 8

lbs. is now far away from the beginning marker of 0 lbs. If you lose another pound, who cares? It won't seem noticeable. On the flipside, 8 lbs. is very close to the specific goal of 10 lbs. Here, losing one extra pound will bring you 50% closer to this goal, which is highly motivating.

It sounds complicated, but the application is simple: Your goals should start broad, and *then* become specific. Some examples:

▶ **Fitness.** In early stages, don't set a specific goal, such as run 5 km, lose 15 lbs., gain 10 lbs. of muscle. Focus on *any* progress. This motion feels more impactful.

▶ **Consulting.** Need to improve your client's bottom line? Fixate their expectations on *any* level of improvement. Eventually mold these expectations into a tangible number.

▶ **Saving Money.** Want to save money this year? Start with a broad goal to save as much as possible. A specific goal, like $3,000, would only increase your spending because every payment would feel small and negligible: *Hmm, can I buy this life-size portrait of Ronald McDonald for $250? Well, $250 is far below my goal of $3,000. So yes.*

Finally, when you eventually transform your goal into a tangible number, you should create a range:

Specific: Lose 10 lbs.
Range: Lose 8–12 lbs.

Ranges bring the goal closer to you, providing the optimal level of challenge: The upper bar gives you something to strive toward, yet the lower bar provides a safety net to catch you (Scott & Nowlis, 2013).

Safety nets are important because you need to reduce the possibility of failure, which can lead to self-sabotage. Perhaps you set a goal to eat fewer than 2,000 calories each day. You might expect that, upon reaching 2001 calories, you would eat less for the remaining day. But you do the opposite; you eat *more* (Soman, & Cheema, 2004). This response is called the what-the-hell effect: *Hmm, I failed to stay under my goal of 2,000 calories. Guess it doesn't matter anymore. What the hell, let's eat this cake.*

∞

Let's briefly recap.

Did you notice that the previous sentence—Let's briefly recap—is really short? This sentence eased your initial motion inside this new section. And now that you've read a few sentences, you possess momentum to continue.

Here's the takeaway: Goals are abstract concepts, so your brain constructs these ideas with tangible concepts. One prominent concept is motion. Whenever you think of a goal, your brain creates this mental picture with sensory motion. Starting a new goal can feel difficult because, according to your brain, you haven't moved yet. You are at rest . . . and objects at rest stay at rest.

You can gain momentum by easing the initial motion:

▶ Endow progress in the beginning
▶ Arrange goals from easy to difficult
▶ Start with broad goals

This progress feels like motion in your brain, giving you the necessary momentum to continue pursuing this goal.

Tweak the Sensory Symbols

Mental pictures can be activated by symbols. Don't let the term "symbol" confuse you; a symbol is anything that identifies a particular behavior or mental picture.

Suppose that you see this task on your calendar:

Go to the gym

Your handwriting is so dreadfully illegible that you can barely distinguish the words, "Go to the gym."

Symbols, such as written tasks, are important because the visual traits can distort the resulting imagery. When you see this task on your calendar, the traits of these words (e.g., messiness) will creep into your mental picture. Going to the gym will seem like a blurry endeavor.

This section will teach you how to tweak symbols so that you instill clearer images.

Ease the Visual Motion of Progress

Imagine that you launched a website, and your visitors need to complete a few steps to create an account. You might depict this progress with a horizontal bar:

This bar is a symbol for the progress, so it activates a mental picture of the remaining tasks. Using some clever tricks, you could design a bar that motivates visitors to complete those tasks. How? Simply create a bar in which the motion feels easy. Visitors will confuse this visual motion for abstract motion: *Hmm, I can imagine this bar moving across the distance. Therefore, these steps must be easy.*

You could:

- ▶ **Start the Progress Above Zero** Endow people with progress for an arbitrary step (e.g., visiting the website).
- ▶ **Choose Bars With an Aerodynamic Shape.** Rounded ovals seem easier to move. Easier motion? Easier tasks.
- ▶ **Shorten the Distance.** A short *visual* distance creates a mental picture of a short *abstract* distance. Same with time notations. Want to make an event seem shorter or longer? Adjust the visual gap between those numbers (e.g., 6–8 PM vs. 6 — 8 PM).

▶ **Shorten the Height.** Thick bars seem slower. Display a thin bar that can easily move across the distance.

▶ **Animate the Motion.** Show the bar actually moving. Thanks to a momentum effect, this bar will seem further ahead.

▶ **Use Horizontal Bars.** Vertical bars are less effective because of gravity: *Hmm, I can't picture this bar moving upward. These steps must be difficult.*[16]

Before we proceed to the next application of motion, let's illustrate this idea with another symbol: size.

Adjust the Visual Size of Numbers

Numbers are abstract concepts, so we learned these ideas by attaching them to a sensory concept. The winner? Spatial size. Whenever you think of a number, like 350, your brain is activating a hidden concept of spatial size—a *smallness* or *largeness*, if you will.

Now, we also created digits—like 350—to symbolize these sizes. Your brain, upon seeing these digits, will envision a smallness or largeness. See the issue? Depending on the context, digits can be *visually* small or large. Suppose that you see 350 in a small font, like ₃₅₀. Your brain will confuse this *visual* size for the *abstract* size: *Hmm, how big is this number? Something feels small. Therefore, this number must be small.*

It's the same effect as messy handwriting, except this new trait—smallness—is creeping into the mental picture.

Want to influence the perception of numbers? Adjust their visual size:

---

[16] Why not display a progress bar that falls downward? Wouldn't this motion seem easier? Okay, let's try it. Right now, envision a progress bar that travels from top to bottom . . . are you picturing it? It feels weird, doesn't it? Why is that? You can blame our sensory reality: When you add objects to a real pile in the sensory world, the pile rises . . . it doesn't fall. You extend this reality into the realm of computers. Oh, and horizontal bars move from left to right because you read from left to right. If your culture reads from right to left, then progress moves from right to left.

▶ **Prices.** Prices seem cheaper in smaller fonts (Coulter & Coulter, 2005). *Hmm, something feels small. It must be the price.*[17]

▶ **Calories.** Food manufacturers are required to enlarge the number of calories on labels. *Hmm, something feels big. This must be a lot of calories. I'll eat less.*

▶ **Time.** A length of time, like 2 hours, could seem shorter or longer depending on the font size: *Hmm, something about this event feels small. It'll be quick.*

Reduce the Visual Size of Tasks

Numbers are just one example; you can adjust the size of *any* symbol. In an episode of *The Office*, Pam created a giant chore wheel to motivate coworkers. Everybody hated it. Yet after she transformed this wheel into a tiny wheel, everybody loved it. She said: "The tiny wheel actually does have chores. It's so cute no one seems to mind."

Think about it. This small chore wheel is symbolizing various behaviors (e.g., vacuuming, cleaning, organizing). Upon seeing a small wheel, your brain injects *smallness* into the resulting mental pictures: *Hmm, how long will it take to vacuum? Something feels small. It won't take long.*

Glance through the table of contents of this book, and you'll notice that each chapter title is deliberately short. Upon seeing these short titles, your brain injects *smallness* into the resulting mental pictures: *Hmm, do I want to read this next chapter? Something feels short and easy. This chapter will be easy to get through.*

Or consider buttons on the computer. A large purchase button could influence your perception: *Hmm, something feels big. Therefore . . .*

    . . . this price must be high.

    . . . the checkout must have a lot of steps.

    . . . this product must offer a lot of value.

A large button could be good or bad; it depends on the traits that

---

[17] You can refer to my YouTube video "The Cognitive Origin of Numbers" to see other examples with prices.

you are evaluating. The product could seem *more* expensive. Or *more* effortful. Or *more* valuable.

Evidence shows that tall people earn higher salaries (Judge & Cable, 2004). Perhaps managers, while interviewing a tall candidate, are injecting *largeness* into abstract traits. Tall people seem *more* responsible. *More* intelligent. *More* ambitious.

Here's the key idea: We use symbols to represent abstract ideas. When you see these symbols, your brain imagines these concepts. Therefore, the traits of these symbols will creep into these mental pictures.

Alright, enough digression. Let's return to motion.

Expand Milestones When Necessary

Objects in motion stay in motion—unless, of course, those objects are acted upon by an external force. While pursuing a goal, your motion will slow down if you collide with an external force.

And, unfortunately, collisions are easier than you think; in fact, it happens every time you achieve a goal or milestone. On rainy days in New York City, for example, data showed that people were having trouble finding cabs. The culprit? With increased demand, drivers were hitting their quotas sooner and quitting for the remaining day (Camerer et al., 1997). Drivers chose to quit (instead of surpassing their quotas) because their motion stopped after hitting this marker.

To sustain your motivation, you need a constant sense of motion. Be careful when approaching the finish line of a goal; you should do something to prolong this motion:

> ▶ **Add a New Goal.** Swiping apps, like Tinder, provide a continuous stream of new goals. In the midst of swiping one person, you can already see the next person in line. They place a new cup in front of you, even before you grab the current cup.
> ▶ **Pull the Current Goal Farther Away.** Instead of placing a new cup on the table, you could pull the existing cup backward. For

example, before lifting weights, I usually warm up on the tread-mill. I usually strive to run 5 minutes, which seems easy (and thus motivating). However, while reaching this goal, I expand it to 10 minutes . . . then 15 minutes.[18]

▶ **Switch Metrics If Necessary.** You might reach a plateau along your goal pursuit. And that's bad. If you stop losing weight, then this slowed motion could reduce your motivation. Perhaps you could switch your metric to something else (e.g., running speed, running distance, number of pushups). Find something that *will* depict progress and motion.

Once you reach the end of this paragraph, you will be reaching the end of this section. You will be completing a milestone, which could slow your motion of reading. Perhaps I should do something to sustain your motion, like leaving a cliffhanger at the end of this paragraph. This cliffhanger might . . .

Set Deadlines in the Same Time Period

. . . nudge you to this new section. Ah, we're here. And hey, you've already read a few sentences. You might as well keep going.

In order to understand this next application, you need to understand another sensory concept: containment.

You live in a sensory world with many physical containers. Consider your breakfast routine—it consists entirely of shifting objects from one container to another. You pour water into a coffee maker; you pour the

---

[18] During an intense run, I'll play a game with myself. When I'm on the verge of quitting, I'll look for a metric on the treadmill that is approaching a concrete number. If I've been running for 14 min and 18 sec, then my goal becomes 15 minutes. While reaching this milestone, I'll find a new goal: If the mileage is showing 1.91 miles, then my new goal is 2 miles. And then I'll find a new goal: If the calorie metric is showing 356, then my goal becomes 375. You can sustain motivation by incrementally expand-ing your goals.

coffee into a mug; you tilt cereal into a bowl; you pour milk into this same bowl; you then move all of these items—coffee, cereal, milk—into a final container: your body.

Containment is everywhere, and it fueled many abstract concepts. For example, the word "in" depicts sensory containment: This book is "in" your hands. Over time, we expanded this word into abstract containment: You can be "in" a good mood. Good moods are entirely intangible, but you can envision this concept as a physical container.

This imagery, albeit subtle, can influence important decisions in your life. Suppose that you're buying a home in the mountains, undecided between Washington and Oregon, and you hear about a big earthquake that happened 200 miles away from both homes.

Experts say that seismic activities could create future disasters (e.g., avalanches, landslides) in surrounding areas, even hundreds of miles away. Which home seems more appealing now?

Since both homes will be affected by the same degree, your choice between Washington or Oregon should have remained unaffected. Yet people consistently choose whichever home is located outside of the state with the earthquake. If the earthquake happened in Washington, people choose Oregon; if it happened in Oregon, people choose Washington (Mishra & Mishra, 2010).

Your brain is conceptualizing geographic regions as physical containers with sensory boundaries. If a disaster is sweeping across Washington, then residents of Oregon will feel safer—even if they live nearby—because the geographic boundary feels like a physical boundary, shielding them from the incoming disaster.

I experienced a similar effect last year when I moved from Boston to Raleigh, North Carolina. While living in Boston, I never wanted to make the 4-hour drive to NYC because it seemed like galaxies away. Yet now, the 4-hour drive to Asheville, another city within North Carolina, seems pretty close . . . even though it's the same distance.

This effect happens with deadlines, too.

Much like boundaries in geography, the boundaries of time—days, weeks, months, years—are built with physical containment. Suppose that you are given 5 days to complete a task. If you receive this task near the end of a month, say April 27, then your deadline will fall in May, which is a different container:

You are near this deadline, but an arbitrary boundary is separating you from it. And thus, this deadline seems less urgent, as if it won't affect you.

Receiving this task a few days sooner, like April 24, would have created a deadline inside April. Even though you would still have 5 days to complete it, your motivation would be higher.

Researchers confirmed this outcome in a series of studies (see Tu & Soman, 2014). Deadlines were motivating in these locations:

▶ **End of Week, Month, or Year.** A deadline "this month" seems closer than a deadline "next month." Even if it's the same duration of time.

▶ **Before a Big Event.** When MBA students were attending a formal dinner later that month, they categorized time in two groups: before the dinner vs. after the dinner. They started a task sooner when this deadline was before the dinner (their current container).

▶ **Visual Groups in a Calendar.** Suppose that today is March 9, and your deadline is March 13. You can distort this deadline through visual grouping in your calendar. In the following image, the deadline on the left seems farther, whereas the deadline on the right seems sooner.

March

M	T	W	Th	F	Sat	Sun
	1	2	3	4	5	6
7	8	9	10	11	12	13
14	15	16	17	18	19	20
21	22	23	24	25	26	27
28	29	30	31			

March

M	T	W	Th	F	Sat	Sun
	1	2	3	4	5	6
7	8	9	10	11	12	13
14	15	16	17	18	19	20
21	22	23	24	25	26	27
28	29	30	31			

∞

This book has focused heavily on the science behind everything, and I realize that some readers might only want the "how" without the "why."

But the underlying science is far more important than the applications. In recent months, a better understanding of this science could have saved tens of thousands of lives. Possibly hundreds of thousands. Possibly more.

I'm writing this chapter in April of 2020, a few months into the global pandemic of COVID-19. And, like many countries, the United States was slow to prepare and respond. Here's a simplified version of events:

China: Things are pretty bad here.
Italy: Well, that's happening in China. It won't happen here.
Things get bad in Italy.

Italy: Things are pretty bad here.
USA: Well, that's happening in Italy. It won't happen here.
Things get bad in the USA.

Governmental decisions, which have life-or-death consequences, are made by humans with flawed brains, brains that are conceptualizing geographic regions with sensory boundaries, thereby failing to grasp the true nature of a rapidly spreading pandemic. With a better understanding of these sensory principles, we could have predicted this inevitable spread and prepared sooner—saving many, many lives.

My goal isn't to fault humans or sound negative. My goal is to articulate the science, even if it seems tedious and unnecessary, because this knowledge can overcome these hidden biases. This knowledge can save lives.

∞

We're approaching the end of this chapter, a metaphorical boundary that could slow your motion. To push you through this boundary, I should do something to boost your motion. But how? I already left a cliffhanger earlier. Let's try something else.

Maybe I could do something with the sensory cues of writing. Maybe I can start adjusting the size of these paragraphs. Notice that the previous paragraph was long? And this new paragraph is shorter?

Sentences are getting shorter, too. You are now reading more paragraphs. And more sentences. In less time. Perhaps you are gaining motion.

Go ahead, I believe in you . . . burst through this boundary.
push

SUMMARY OF MOTION

Your brain uses sensory motion to conceptualize progress. You can boost motivation through a sense of motion,
such as experiencing an early win or expanding goals
while approaching the finish line. This motion gives you
the necessary momentum to continue pursuing the goal.

Cross Out Completed Milestones

Do you feel oddly satisfied after crossing out an item on your to-do list?
This visual completion depicts your progress and motion across your
list of tasks. Don't rob your brain of this experience—whenever you
complete a task, cross it out and savor the pleasure.

Capture Attention With Dynamic Imagery

Images capture more attention when they depict motion (Cian,
Krishna, & Elder, 2015). The warning sign on the right could capture
more attention (and save lives). This application seems irrelevant to
the chapter, but it relates to the next point.

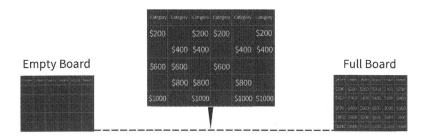

Capture Attention With Causal Motion

Motion captures attention, right? On Netflix, I noticed that the thumbnail for *Jeopardy!* was a partially empty board of questions, as if this photo were taken from the middle of a game. This thumbnail, even though it's devoid of sensory motion, still has causal motion; this board is moving from full to empty. Therefore, a partially-empty board should capture more attention because sensory motion is lurking underneath.

Close Small Debt Accounts First

Do you have multiple accounts in which you owe money? Start by closing the smaller accounts. This momentum will ease your ability to close the larger accounts (Gal & McShane, 2012).

Use Shrinking Motion in Scarcity Appeals

To the untrained eye, those messages seem identical. But if you look closely, the second message is more persuasive because motion is shrinking: A handful of 50 discounts are reducing to zero. Customers feel more compelled to pounce on those discounts before they disappear.

Your Boss	New Project	Hi Nick, We're starting a new task...
Some Marketer	**MAJOR DISCOUNT. GET IT NOW!!!!!**	#$@%&...
Ex from Church	Whatchu Doing?	Just thinking of you and God...
Leo DiCaprio	Stop Contacting Me	How did you get my info...

Use Short Subject Lines in Emails

Recipients confuse the smallness of a subject line with the amount of work in reading the email: *Hmm, should I open this email? How long will it take? Something feels short. It'll be quick.*

Your Boss	New Project	Hi Nick, We're starting a new task...
Some Marketer	**MAJOR DISCOUNT. GET IT NOW!!!!!**	#$@%&...
Ex from Church	Whatchu Doing?	Just thinking of you and God...
Leo DiCaprio	Stop Contacting Me	How did you get my info...

Give a Preview of Content

In most email clients, you can usually see the beginning of an email. This preview extracts a small amount of motion, building your momentum to open the email. Many newspapers follow the same strategy with online articles; they display the beginning portion of an article before asking you to subscribe.

7

Grouping

HOW MANY OBJECTS do you see below?

Three objects, right?
Okay, what about now:

Hmm . . . it's different now, isn't it? Sure, you see three circles . . . but your brain is grouping two circles on the left, as if they were a single object.

In reality, the concept of an "object" is entirely fluid. You're not holding a single book right now; you're holding *many* objects. Think about it. This book is divided into chapters; those chapters have paragraphs; those paragraphs have sentences; those sentences have words; those words have letters. This book, in terms of letters, has roughly 300,000 objects.

And we could drill deeper. Some letters contain multiple objects, like the lowercase *i* with its dot above. If we wanted, we could conceptualize this dot with two halves:

Suddenly that dot has two objects. And we could keep dividing this dot into *more* units: fourths, eights, sixteenths. No matter how many divisions we create, we could always create more units by dividing this number in half. And again. And again. In other words, this book—*the mere object that you're holding in your hands*—contains an infinite number of objects . . . the same number of objects that you'd find on earth itself.

Here's the point: The boundaries of an object are entirely flexible, so *anything*—technically—could be an object. That idea has profound implications, as you'll discover in this chapter.

∞

Objects have flexible boundaries, so then . . . what *is* an object? When do you perceive items as a cohesive unit?

The answer: *Gestalt principles.*

Gestalt principles tell us when we are more likely to group items into a single entity.

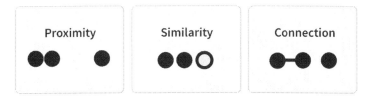

Look around you. Your brain is grouping the world into various entities. This book has 100+ pages, yet it *seems* like one object. A highlighter has a detachable cap, yet it *seems* like one object. The word "object" has six letters, yet it *seems* like one object. You can perceive *anything* to be an object, thanks to Gestalt principles.

And now it gets interesting.

Imagine that you see the following products on a store shelf: hot sauce, crackers, mayonnaise, and beans.

Consciously, you can distinguish these foods. Subconsciously, however, you group the crackers and mayonnaise because of their proximity in the middle. Your brain doesn't see crackers *and* mayonnaise. It sees one entity: Crayonnaise. Or some weird combination.

This grouping triggers a devious effect, in which the traits of each food are fusing together: Mayonnaise inherits traits from the crackers, while the crackers inherit traits from the mayonnaise. What kind of traits? Surveys indicate that mayonnaise can seem disgusting; therefore, those crackers—which are grouped with the mayonnaise—will seem more disgusting (Morales & Fitzsimons, 2007).

I call this principle *convergent processing* or simply *convergence.* When you group items into a single entity, the new entity inherits the qualities of each component; the traits are fusing together into this new object.[19]

Let's look at one final example, and then we'll explore the profound implications of this principle.

---

[19] See Chapter 4 of *The Tangled Mind* for the detailed mechanism.

Isolate Indulgent Options

On your coffee table, you see a gossip magazine resting on a textbook:

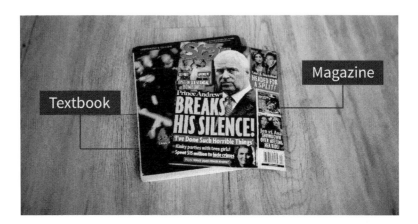

First problem: The gossip magazine is lying on top. You can imagine grabbing this magazine instead of the textbook

Second problem: Unless you're a mega nerd like me, who uses words like mega, and who prefers to read textbooks, then you will likely opt for the gossip magazine in default scenarios. You need a rational motive—guilt, obligation, reward—to choose the textbook.

Well, do you see the issue?

The magazine and textbook are touching each other, so your brain is merging these items into a single entity. You no longer feel guilty reading the gossip magazine because this magazine is inheriting a rational essence from the textbook. This choice *feels* more responsible.

Researchers confirmed this idea: Participants preferred a DVD set of *Friends* when it was lying on top of an economics textbook because this choice *seemed* more responsible (Fishbach & Zhang, 2008).

Those researchers conducted other studies with food, and they found similar results:

▶ **Food Trays.** Students were more likely to choose a piece of chocolate when it was lying on the same tray as an apple.

▶ **Pages in a Menu.** Unhealthy food seemed healthier when these options were displayed on the same page as healthy food.

You could extend this effect to anything:

▶ **Divisions in a Freezer.** My freezer is separated into two bins. If I place ice cream inside the same bin as frozen vegetables, my brain will group the ice cream and vegetables. The ice cream will seem healthier, and I'll be tempted to eat it.
▶ **Separate Cabinets.** Don't keep healthy food inside the same cabinet as unhealthy food. Otherwise you will inject a "healthy" essence into those unhealthy foods.

The takeaway: Isolate bad choices from good choices so that you prevent your brain from injecting a good essence into those bad choices.

Group Yourself With Objects

The term "object" implies a lifeless object (e.g., mayonnaise, textbook, ice cream). But in reality, people are objects. YOU are an object. And thus, not only can your brain group magazines and textbooks, but it can also expand the boundaries of your physical body to include other entities.

In his comedy special *23 Hours to Kill*, Jerry Seinfeld describes our intense attachment to phones, as if phones have become part of our physical bodies:

> We are not separating from the phone. It's a part of us now . . . That's why it's called an iPhone: it's half myself, half phone. That's a complete individual . . . the only reason people still exist is phones need pockets to ride around in.

This convergence, I'm arguing, is actually happening. We spend so much time with our phones that our brains are expanding the boundaries of our physical bodies to include them inside our identity. Removing this possession can feel as painful as removing a finger.

Let's illustrate this idea. This next request will sound weird, but stick with me.

Remember how the world contains an infinite number of objects? And you can categorize these objects in any way? Right now, categorize the world into two objects: yourself and everything else. In other words, focus on your physical body. Are you doing it? Okay, now focus on everything else in the world besides your body . . . and now refocus on your body again. Keep shifting back-and-forth between your body and everything else—I know it seems weird, but this idea is important.

Done?

Now, be honest, when you focused on your physical body, were you conceptualizing your body as naked? Or, like most people, were you including your clothes inside this focus?

Your clothes *should* have been part of "everything else" in the world, but your brain—I suspect—was grouping your clothes with your physical body. You just experienced convergence first-hand. You and your clothing, according to your brain, were a single entity; and thus, you inherited traits from your clothing.

So, what clothes are you wearing? And, more importantly, what do you think of these clothes? Maybe you're wearing counterfeit sunglasses. Could these traits—deceit, insincerity, immorality—merge with your identity? Would you be more likely to perform immoral behaviors, like cheating on a test? It sounds crazy, but that's what happened in one study (Gino, Norton, & Ariely, 2010).

It's not just cellphones and clothing. Do you have any favorite brands? Brands that you frequently use? Then those traits—the creative traits of Apple, the rugged traits of Harley Davidson, the visionary traits of Tesla, the courageous traits of Red Bull—are fusing with your identity. You *are* what you *have*.

Strangely, this effect might have changed my life. In my early twenties, I worked as a Marketing Research Analyst, and I was the spinning image of the dorky "PC guy" in the classic Apple commercial: *Hi, I'm a Mac . . . and I'm a PC.* I had, indeed, always used a PC, but I switched to a Mac shortly after leaving that job, for a reason that escapes my memory. Fast forward to this moment, I've been using my Mac laptop for 10+ hours every day. For years. And during that time, my interests have drastically changed. Today, I work on many design projects—video, web, graphics—that I never could have pictured in my PC days. I now think of myself as a creative, instead of a business person, and I find myself searching for the true cause of this transformation: Did I buy a Mac because I always wanted to be a creative? Or did I become a creative *because* of my Mac?

Analyze the possessions in your life to see how they might be affecting you. Still hanging onto the love letters from your ex? Or an embarrassing video of your flubbed presentation? Why? Get rid of them—that negativity is oozing into your identity. Marie Kondo had the right idea with her method of tidying up: If something doesn't spark joy, then throw it away.

∞

Not only do we inherit traits from our possessions, but our possessions also inherit traits from us. Can't seem to throw away your antiquated CD collection? Or that baby blanket from childhood? Those "close" possessions are part of your identity. Part of *you.*

That grouping mechanism, I suspect, is the main culprit behind a popular principle in economics called the *endowment effect.* Suppose that I have a mug. How much would you pay for it? $3.00? $4.00? Let's say $3.50.

Now, reverse the scenario. Suppose that *you* have a mug. And I'm trying to buy it. How much would you sell it for? Rationally, this amount should be the same: $3.50. But in reality, studies show that participants need more money, like $6.00, to depart with it (Kahneman, Knetsch, & Thaler, 1990).

Immediately after owning something, you place more value on it because this object has become part of your identity, inheriting pieces and remnants of you. You *are* the mug. And thus, you need more money to depart with it. It seems like a cutesy principle, but this endowment effect creates a pervasive discrepancy between buyers and sellers in our economic paradigm. And you'll see other implications later.

For now, you can increase somebody's desire for an object by injecting this object with aspects of their identity. You could:

- ▶ **Attach a Photo.** Marketers often ask you to upload a profile photo to their digital platform. This photo is often visible on every page of their software, usually in the top-right corner. This photo injects the software with your identity, enhancing your affinity toward it. Clever marketers do this even in platforms where nobody else will ever see this photo.
- ▶ **Get People to Touch.** Apple stores modernized the concept of retail by letting customers touch and interact with all of their products, instilling a feeling of ownership (see Brasel & Gips, 2014).
- ▶ **Ask People to Help With Outcomes.** Do your children hate vegetables? Ask them to help with a small garden occasionally. This garden (and vegetables) will become *theirs*, injecting these vegetables with their identity. When families participated in a community garden that grew vegetables, overweight children lowered their BMI because they ate more vegetables (Castro, Samuels, Harman, 2013). This effect happens with adults, too. Adults prefer self-made products; it's called the *IKEA effect* (Nortion, Mochon, & Ariely, 2012).

Finally, consider this book. This book was birthed from my brain. It's part of me. Part of my identity. I could pretend that I'm a rational human being with a tough exterior, imperviable to a 1-star review on Amazon . . . but I'd be lying. Negative feedback *will* affect me. When people "pour their heart and soul" into something, they are literally injecting this creation with remnants of their identity. Any comments—good or bad—become infused with the creator. The creator *is* the creation.

Obviously, we shouldn't censor opinions for the sake of coddling sensitive creators, but moving forward, stop and reflect before you harshly criticize somebody's work. Is a friend asking you to read their novel? Or watch their film? Or view their artwork? It's easy to spew criticism when the work means nothing to you—but for the creator, it could mean everything. Your words will be interpreted in terms of their identity. Be honest . . . yet mindful.

Group Yourself With People

You just learned that we group ourselves with close possessions. Did you notice the metaphor of proximity? We call them "close" possessions because our brain conceives them to be physically close to us.

You merge with those possessions because of a hidden principle of proximity deep in your subconscious.

Still with me?

You find the same metaphor with social relationships: You are "close" to certain people, even though you might act "distant" occasionally. Deep in your brain, any "close" relationship is conceptualized with proximity:

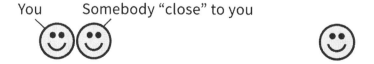

Again, *anything* can be an object. Your brain doesn't care about the physical boundaries around your body; it can expand these boundaries to encapsulate other entities. If you feel "close" to somebody, then your brain is grouping yourself with this person. You become a single entity.

Self-help experts claim that you become the average of the five people that you spend the most time with. This statement is more literal than we thought. The more time that you spend with someone, the closer you become. The closer you become, the more your brain expands your boundaries to encapsulate this person inside your identity, instilling any traits of this person—good or bad—inside you. You *become* this person.

You can see evidence with studies on goal contagion. Suppose that you're an American football coach in this situation:

> You're winning by 17 points. It's 4th quarter with a few seconds left, and you have 1st down on the opponent's 15-yard line. How much do you want to score another touchdown?

Researchers at Ohio State University used that question to measure the competitiveness of students. In that scenario, your team doesn't need to score another touchdown; you'll win the game regardless. Thus, anybody who wants to score another touchdown is feeling more competitive.

Those researchers examined how people answered this question after viewing a racquetball match between two people, either a competitive match (e.g., fast swings) or cooperative match (e.g., slow swings).

Now, you might be thinking: *If students watched a competitive match, then they probably answered that football question more competitively.* And sure, that's *nearly* correct. But there was a necessary condition: Participants needed to believe that these racquetball players were fellow students at their school—that is, they needed to see "Ohio State University" in the video (Loersch et al., 2008).

The gist of the study: Participants became more competitive after viewing a racquetball match in which the players, fellow students at the same school, were competitive.

Hold this thought.

In the previous chapter, I discussed how abstract categories (e.g., days, weeks, months) are conceptualized as physical containers in your brain.

Well, containment is another Gestalt principle. Objects inside a container seem like a single entity:

And that's why participants in the study behaved more competitively. If the racquetball players were fellow students at the same school, this "social group" was conceptualized as a physical container, merging everyone into a single entity.

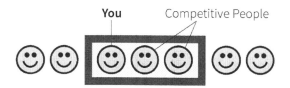

Social groups are powerful because we merge with the other people inside these containers. Participants in the previous study inherited the competitive traits of fellow students.

Think about your life.

Who do you spend the most time with? Whoever these people are, you will be "close" to them. And your brain will be grouping your identity with those people. So, what are they like? Competitive? Lazy? Ambitious? Kind? Those traits will become *your* traits.

Be careful with your inner circle. Choose people that will bring positive value into your life. Or, if you're stuck with somebody negative, then occasionally reflect on your inherent differences. Your brain *can* distinguish the boundaries between you . . . it just takes more effort.

Before ending the chapter, let's explore one final application of grouping: empathy.

∞

Humans are selfish creatures, but it's not our fault . . . we *needed* to be selfish in order to survive the barbaric nature of early times.

This selfishness, an innate part of human nature, can pose a mystery in today's world: If humans are inherently selfish, then why do we care for other people? Why do we feel empathy? Wouldn't empathy *reduce* our survival in early times? Anyone who sacrificed themselves for another person wouldn't live long enough to endow their children with this empathy gene.

Some researchers argue that we acquired empathy through tribal relationships: We needed to protect our tribe so that our tribe would protect us. And sure, that could play a role. But I want to propose, what I consider to be, a more plausible explanation for the origin of empathy. Or perhaps the mechanism that spurred our tribal empathy.

You feel empathy for other people because, deep in your subconscious, your brain is expanding the boundaries of your physical body to include other people inside your identity. You care for other people because, according to your brain, you *are* those people.

When you peel back the layers of empathy, you find striking coincidences with grouping. Every aspect of empathy can be traced to a Gestalt principle:

- ▶ **Proximity.** The "closer" you feel to somebody, the more you empathize with this person. It even happens with spatial proximity: If somebody dies across the world, then you don't blink an eye; but if somebody dies across the street—even if you knew neither person—you feel more empathy for the spatially closer person.
- ▶ **Similarity.** You feel empathy for people who are similar to you. And this empathy rises in accordance with the morphological similarity to human bodies—that is, your empathy rises across this sequence: worms, fish, amphibians, reptiles, birds, mammals, primates, humans (Harrison & Hall, 2010). Many people have

no qualms eating a lobster, but everybody has qualms eating a human. We feel this jolting reaction because it feels like we are eating ourselves.

▶ **Common Motion.** If you see two dots moving in tandem, you group them as a unit. Similarly, you exhibit a *chameleon effect*, in which you show more empathy toward people who subtly mimic your body language (Chartrand & Bargh, 1999). This mimicry creates a synchronous unit between both bodies, causing your brain to group yourself with these people.

In the deep abyss of your brain, there are Gestalt principles from the sensory world—proximity, similarity, common motion, connection, containment—that are binding disparate items into a single unit, influencing your perception and behavior. Even important behaviors, like empathy:

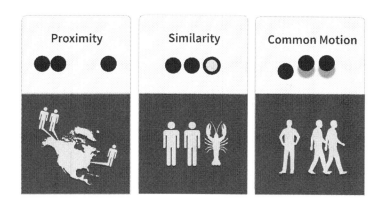

Instead of ignoring the selfish history of our ancestors, we should acknowledge and embrace it; this selfishness blossomed into our modern-day altruism and empathy. Our brains have expanded the boundaries of our bodies to include other people inside our identity. We care for other people *because* we care for ourselves.

And, if this explanation *is* the culprit behind empathy, we can use this knowledge to create *more* empathy in society. I discuss those societal applications in Appendix A.

Place Assurances Near Buttons

Buttons are symbols for a particular behavior. Suppose that you see a purchase button with positive statements directly below. When you see this button and envision the purchase, those nearby benefits will creep into your mental picture (and paint a more desirable image).

Delete Embarrassing Texts

Whoops, wrong number? Delete any embarrassing texts from your phone to block these negative emotions from entering your identity.

A		
12-Month Lease	$1,250
Month-to-Month	$1,750

B		
12-Month Lease	**$1,250**
Month-to-Month	**$1,750**

C		
12-Month Lease	$1,250
Month-to-Month	$1,750

Visually Group Numbers

I received a letter to renew my apartment lease, and it displayed prices using Format A. Suppose that we added a background color to the column (Format B). This design is grouping (and thus merging) these prices into an average: $1,250 seems higher, while $1,750 seems lower. Format C triggers the opposite effect: $1,250 seems lower, while $1,750 seems higher because these prices are polarizing away from each other. You can visually group (or separate) numbers, depending on the options that you want people to choose.

Extend the Boundaries of Your Service

Many ATMs place carpets in front, which reduces the perceived waiting time (Zhao, Lee, & Soman, 2012). When you reach this carpet, it feels like you reached the ATM because your brain is grouping this carpet with the ATM.

Let People Choose the Reward

Most businesses motivate salespeople through commissions, but why not let them choose an incentive: commission, vacation days, remote days, or something else. These incentives will be a closer match with their true desire (e.g., some might prefer money, while others might prefer vacation days). Plus, the mere act of choosing will inject the chooser's identity into this incentive (and it will become more enticing).

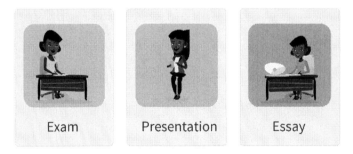

Let People Choose the Task

Likewise, teachers could let students choose the type of assignment: take an exam, deliver a presentation, or write an essay.

VS "Millions of People"

Humanize the Traits of People

You are more likely to donate money to help an African girl named Rokia compared to the same request to help "millions of people" (which would include Rokia). You can blame a mixture of vividness and grouping. Identifiable traits—name, age, picture—create a vivid mental picture, easing your ability to group with this person. It's easy to converge with a person; it's difficult to converge with a statistic.

8

Balance

LEAN YOUR BODY to the left.

How do you feel? Weird, right? Your brain is probably confused and annoyed: "Hey, what are you doing? Sit upright."

You constantly desire a state of physical balance, an equilibrium that can only be achieved through a yin and yang mechanism: A movement on one side requires a movement on the opposing side.

Lean to the left? You want to lean right.

Lean to the right? You want to lean left.

You've been feeling this sensation from the moment that you ventured into this world, and this experience fueled many future concepts.

One concept is ambivalence. Sometimes a decision will have positive *and* negative consequences; you often hear the phrase: *On one hand . . . on the other hand.* Turns out, this abstract wavering leads to bodily wavering: While reading an article with positive and negative arguments, people shifted their weight from side-to-side. The reverse happened, too: Shifting their weight from side-to-side instilled more mixed feelings (Schneider et al., 2013).

Or consider stability. Have you ever described a career as stable? How about a relationship? Careers and relationships are disconnected from the sensory world, yet you conceive these ideas with physical stability. People who felt physically unstable (e.g., standing on one foot, sitting in a wobbly chair) believed that their relationships would end sooner: *Hmm, how long will my relationship last? Something feels unstable. It must be my relationship* (Forest et al., 2015; Kille, Forest, & Wood, 2013).

Here's the takeaway: Your brain is constantly craving physical balance. This experience is so primitive and pervasive that you injected this sensory idea into many concepts. We've seen two concepts, ambivalence and stability, but this chapter will propose a third concept: fairness.

It's no coincidence that a "fair" decision seems *equitable* or *just* or . . . drum roll . . . *balanced*. In this chapter, I'll argue that sensory balance constructed the human idea of fairness, and—by extension—all of the societal endeavors (e.g., criminal justice system) that are built upon on this idea. If we understand the true origin of fairness, then we can spot instances where this fundamental idea, an idea that *seems* universal, might actually be erroneous. Just because humans crave balance in the sensory world doesn't mean that humans should derive the concept of "fairness" from this sensory idea, imputing the same physical laws.

This chapter has broad implications, but I'll stay focused on motivation. And I'll try to keep my arguments fair and balanced.

Err . . . fair and . . . optimal?

The Equity Scale

The next concept might be the most complex idea in the book, but I'll try to simplify things.

I categorized all behaviors into four types—based on valence (*good* or *bad*) and agency (*doing* or *receiving*).

Just to clarify:

- ▶ **Misdeed:** You do a bad behavior (e.g., punch someone).
- ▶ **Mishaps:** You receive a bad behavior (e.g., get punched).
- ▶ **Obligation:** You do a good behavior (e.g., donate money).
- ▶ **Enrichment:** You receive a good behavior (e.g., win money).

Typically, YOU determine the category. If your boss is forcing you to read this book, then this behavior could feel like a mishap or obligation.

If you stole this book, then this identical behavior could feel like a misdeed. Same behavior. Different category. It all depends on your perception.

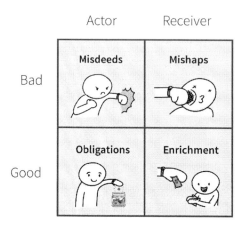

Still with me?

I'll swap the bottom two behaviors—obligations and enrichment—which will simplify the next explanation. Imagine that this revised matrix is resting upon a fulcrum. I call it the *equity scale*.

The Equity Scale

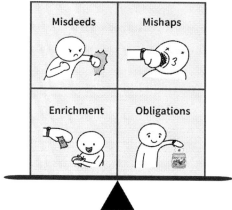

Much like your brain strives for balance in the sensory world, your brain strives for balance in this framework. Any behavior tilts the scale toward the left or right. Then your brain feels an urge for a behavior on the opposing side to regain balance.

Since that scale has two directions—left or right—we find two forces that profoundly influence our behavior: *immunity* and *absolution*.

Immunity

Mishaps and obligations appear on the right. If you experience one of these behaviors, you tilt the scale toward the right, requiring behaviors on the left—misdeeds or enrichment—to regain balance.

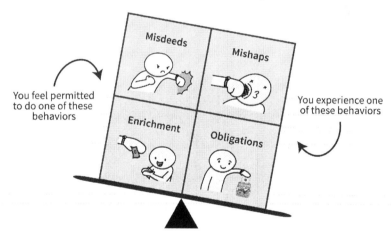

In simple terms: If something bad happens to you or if you do something good, you gain karma to spend. You feel entitled to a reward or permitted to do something bad.

Some examples:

▶ **You Do Something Good? You Can Do Something Bad.** Did you bring reusable bags to a grocery store? You are more likely to buy ice cream (Karmarkar & Bollinger, 2015). You feel permitted to buy ice cream (misdeed) because of your good action (obligation).

▶ **Something Bad Happen to You? You Can Do Something Bad.**

At a particular daycare, parents were frequently late to pick up their children. Managers tried to correct this behavior through a monetary fine, yet this fine only made it worse: parents became tardier (Gneezy & Rustichini, 2000). Parents viewed this fine as a mishap, which balanced their misdeed of tardiness.

I could give evidence for each pathway in the framework, but I don't want to complicate things. If you want a deeper dive, you can refer to Chapter 18 in *The Tangled Mind*, which is densely packed with studies.

Absolution

Misdeeds and enrichment appear on the left. If you experience one of these behaviors, you tilt the scale toward the left, requiring behaviors on the right—mishaps or obligations—to regain balance.

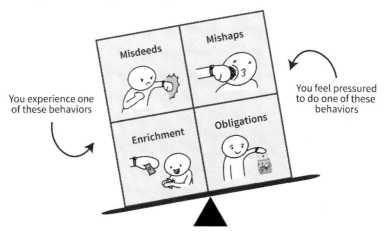

In simple terms: If you do something bad or if something good happens to you, your karma is running a deficit and you need to boost it. You feel compelled to do something good or suffer a negative consequence. Some examples:

▶ **You Do Something Bad? Something Bad Must Happen to You.** When people reflected on an immoral behavior from their past, they held their arm in ice water for a longer duration, as if to punish themselves for the wrongdoing (Bastian, Jetten, & Fasoli, 2011).

▶ **Something Good Happen to You? You Need to Do Something Good.** Reciprocity is a common principle of influence. If somebody helps you, this favor (enrichment) tilts your scale to the left, pressuring you to repay this favor (obligation).

Okay, your brain is probably annoyed at me for throwing so much information at you. The equity scale might sound complicated, but it's very simple if you look at the illustration. Any behavior on one side of the scale will require a behavior on the opposing side.[20]

This chapter will fixate on misdeeds, which are behaviors that make you feel guilty (e.g., eating cake, smoking cigarettes, stealing money). Misdeeds tilt your scale to the left, requiring mishaps or obligations for balance. Using this idea, we can predict when and why we succumb to these temptations (and how to overcome them).

Notice Your Justification of Misdeeds

Remember your ice cream debacle in Chapter 5? You devoured a full carton of ice cream, and you promised yourself that you would start eating healthy.

Okay, it's the next day. You're sitting at your desk, completing an expense report, when you see coworkers flocking to the conference room.

It's Donna's birthday. And there's cake.

You enter the conference room, and you see a stunningly decadent cake staring into your soul.

Enter: your inner voice.

---

[20] We still need research to validate whether the equity scale emerges from physiological balance. I suspect that this framework is only coincidentally related to balance. Nevertheless, if these compulsions *are* emerging from physiological sensations, then this insight would open the door to new applications.

Your rational brain is resisting this cake, yet your emotional brain is frantically searching for excuses to justify eating it:

. . . *I'll start dieting tomorrow.*

. . . *I exercised this morning.*

. . . *I had a rough week.*

Beneath the surface, those excuses are your attempts to regain balance in your equity scale. Eating this cake, a misdeed, will be tilting your scale to the left. Your excuses are trying to correct this imbalance.

I categorized these excuses into five types:

1. **Weaker Misdeed**—This misdeed is so small that it doesn't tilt your scale: "*It's only a small piece of cake.*"
2. **Misdeed is Obligation**—This misdeed is an admirable behavior: "*It's carrot cake, so . . . that's healthy.*"
3. **Separate Obligation**—You did (or will do) something good to balance this misdeed: "*I worked hard today . . . I deserve it.*"
4. **Separate Mishap**—Something bad has happened (or will happen) to balance this misdeed: "*Next week will be rough. Let me enjoy it now.*"
5. **Lack of Agency**—This behavior isn't a misdeed because it wasn't your choice: "*John handed me a piece.*"

It's like a game of whack-a-mole: Once you squash one excuse, another excuse pops up. And those excuses are often meaningless. It's not *really* about the healthiness of carrot cake. Or that John handed you a piece. Or anything else that your inner voice throws at you. Your brain has already decided that it wants cake; you are merely searching for *any* justification to balance this misdeed.

Let's walk through another scenario, and you'll see how these excuses are influencing many decisions—*important decisions*—in your life.

∞

Your two friends just got married.

Now that the wedding is over, you're heading to the nearby

reception, an event that will be ripe with temptations. This section will illustrate how the equity scale influences all of your decisions, small and big.

Eating Wedding Cake

As you enter the reception hall, you see a familiar temptation: a decadent wedding cake. I included this example again to illustrate the sheer variety of excuses that you might hear. Upon seeing this beautiful cake, your inner voice might say:

- ▶ **Weaker Misdeed:** *"One piece won't kill me."*
- ▶ **Misdeed is Obligation:** *"It'll go to waste if I don't eat it."*
- ▶ **Separate Obligation:** *"I'll start dieting tomorrow."*
- ▶ **Separate Mishap:** *"I fumbled my speech. I need consoling."*
- ▶ **Lack of Agency:** *"My whole table is leaving to grab a piece."*

Those excuses help your brain counterbalance the guilt of eating cake. And, in this scenario, your inner voice happens to win. You succumb to this temptation and grab a piece of cake.

Drinking

Today is officially two weeks after you quit drinking. Yet . . . you see the champagne in front of you. Your rational brain wants to chuck it across the room, but your emotional brain is racing to find something—*anything*—that can balance this misdeed:

- ▶ **Weaker Misdeed:** *"It's only one drink."*
- ▶ **Misdeed is Obligation:** *"I need to drink or else I'll be boring."*
- ▶ **Separate Obligation:** *"I've been good . . . I haven't had a drink in two weeks."*
- ▶ **Separate Mishap:** *"Oh, no . . . Taylor is here. I need a drink."*
- ▶ **Lack of Agency:** *"It'll look weird if I don't drink it."*

One drink seems innocent, but it creates a domino effect that leads to *many* drinks. Why? Because one drink feels like a failure. This failure feels like a mishap. And this mishap can counterbalance the misdeed of your second drink, establishing a vicious cycle. It's our old friend, the what-the-hell effect: *I already had one drink. What the hell, let's get wasted.*

But no! You hear those tantalizing excuses, yet you power through them. You offer the champagne to someone nearby, and you pat yourself on the back, unaware that this good action will counterbalance bad actions later tonight.

Frivolous Spending

Everybody at your table heads to the dance floor, but you stay behind. Your dancing quota requires a minimum of two drinks.

To keep yourself occupied, you start browsing your phone—an innocent behavior for most people, yet a hazardous endeavor for someone whose purchase history includes a life-size portrait of Ronald McDonald. You've been trying to curb your spending, but you keep admiring a swanky pair of designer jeans that are screaming your name.

Unfortunately, marketers are clever. On the web page for those swanky jeans, those marketers are becoming your inner voice, using language that helps you overcome this internal struggle. Here are all of the subtle phrases on this web page that are nudging you toward the purchase.

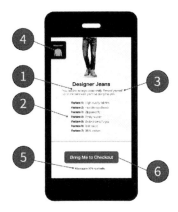

1. **Weaker Misdeed:** *"You need to splurge occasionally."*

Translation: *Go ahead, it's not a big deal . . . you can buy them . . . it won't tilt your scale.*

Also, evidence confirms that assertive language (e.g., you "need" to splurge) is effective for emotional products because people convince themselves that they didn't have a choice (Kronrod, Grinstein, Wathieu, 2012).

2. **Misdeed is Obligation:** *"Feature 1, Feature 2, etc."*

Translation: *Look at the sheer number of attributes . . . these jeans are useful and justified. Don't feel guilty.*

People are more likely to buy emotional products if they see *more* features because these products seem more rational (Sela & Berger, 2012).

3. **Separate Obligation:** *"Reward yourself for the hard work that you will do this year."*

Translation: *You are justified in buying these jeans because you will make up for them later.*

You can sense that a devious marketer wrote that phrase because of the focus toward the future—that is, all of the hard work that you *will* do. Thanks to the *optimism bias* and *planning fallacy*, we overestimate the amount of work that we will accomplish in the future (see Zhang, Fishbach, & Dhar, 2007). Future work will seem bigger than past work that you have already done.

4. **Separate Obligation:** *"Still want this sweatshirt?"*

Translation: *Here's a product that you viewed in the past, but you didn't buy. See that restraint? Good job. Reward yourself now.*

Indeed, people are more likely to buy products after reflecting on a past occasion where they didn't buy (Mukhopadhyay & Johar, 2009).

5. **Separate Obligation:** *"We donate 10% to charity."*

Translation: *Your purchase will be helping the world. If anything, you're a monster if you don't buy these jeans.*
Charity incentives are more effective for emotional products because they counterbalance the guilt (Strahilevitz & Myers, 1998).

6. **Lack of Autonomy:** *"Bring Me to Checkout"*

Translation: *Just stay right there. Don't do anything. We'll do the dirty deed for you.*
I've never seen this text inside a button, but perhaps it would influence your decision. A button such as "Buy" instills a mental picture in which you are the actor. *You* are committing this misdeed. However, a button that says "Bring Me to the Checkout" instills a mental picture in which somebody else is forcing your hand . . . so you shouldn't feel guilty.

With emotional products, like designer jeans, marketers are less focused on *selling* them. Rather, they are focused on *justifying* them.
Yet, despite those psychological triggers, you manage to resist. You slip your phone back inside your pocket before changing your mind.
You have now resisted two tempting behaviors: drinking and spending. These "obligations" have tilted your equity scale toward the right, creating an imbalance. These good actions have given you some immunity for bad actions. So, let's keep progressing.

Cheating on Partner

Immediately after slipping your phone inside your pocket, a stranger sits down at the table.
"Hi, I'm Riley. Did you come here solo too?"

Indeed, you had. Jamie, the person you've been dating for two months, was busy. But you decide to gloss over the subject of Jamie.

"No, I came with the chair. Cute couple, aren't we?"

"Oh, I'm sorry," Riley retorted. "You both look lovely. I'm sure that you chair-ish each other very much."

You and Riley stare at each other, while hiding grins.

"Chair puns already?" you reply. "I won't take that sitting down."

Both of you continue flirting for a couple hours, gradually increasing the overtness. Your rational brain knows that your behavior is wrong, yet your emotional brain keeps firing excuses:

▶ **Weaker Misdeed:** *"I haven't dated Jamie for that long."*
▶ **Misdeed is Obligation:** *"I'll hurt Riley if I don't reciprocate."*
▶ **Separate Obligation:** *"I've never cheated on anyone before."*
▶ **Separate Mishap:** *"Jamie lied to me the other day."*
▶ **Lack of Agency:** *"Riley was hitting on me."*

At the end of the night, you find yourself sitting in Riley's hotel room. Your inner voice has won this battle.

Before you know it, you run into the final decision of the night.

Unprotected Sex

Both of you consent to sex. Shortly afterward, both of you face another decision: whether or not to use a condom.

Your rational brain has always told yourself to be careful in these situations, yet in this moment, you realize that this decision is tougher than you anticipated. Do you have enough willpower?

I've been using gender-neutral names, but imagine that Riley is a female. At this point, both people might be generating their own internal excuses to justify skipping the condom.

Inner voice of male:

- ▶ **Weaker Misdeed:** *"It'll only be this one time."*
- ▶ **Misdeed is Obligation:** *"If I get a condom, I'll lose my erection."*
- ▶ **Separate Obligation:** *"I'll grab a condom next time."*
- ▶ **Separate Mishap:** *"Jamie should have been here tonight."*
- ▶ **Lack of Agency:** *"I don't think Riley wants to use a condom."*

Meanwhile, the inner voice of Riley is firing her own excuses:

- ▶ **Weaker Misdeed:** *"Everybody does it . . . it's not a big deal."*
- ▶ **Misdeed is Obligation:** *"I need to get over my breakup."*
- ▶ **Separate Obligation:** *"I've been careful in the past."*
- ▶ **Separate Mishap:** *"My ex shouldn't have been a jerk."*
- ▶ **Lack of Agency:** *"I don't think he wants to use a condom."*

Those excuses can be dangerously persuasive. They can lead us to make decisions that we know are wrong. Decisions that, deep down, we truly don't want to do; yet, for some reason, we succumb to these excuses.

How can you resist these excuses in the future? The next section will give you practical strategies, but this past section has already given you an incredibly powerful tool: awareness. Reading this chapter has destroyed your ability to continue believing these excuses. Next time that you hear these excuses—and you *will* hear them again—you can no longer plead ignorant. You will know the truth. And you can stop yourself from falling into this trap.

But it's one thing to *notice* excuses; it's another thing to *resist* them. The next section will give you practical techniques to overcome them.

Prevent Your Justification of Misdeeds

Most misdeeds involve an emotional decision, but why do humans feel emotions in the first place?

Across evolution, we acquired emotions because these feelings helped us make faster decisions (Chang & Tuan Pham, 2013). If you saw a tiger in close proximity, then a strong emotion helped you make a faster decision (and thus survive). These evolutionary circumstances infused emotions with proximity: The closer a stimulus, the stronger your emotions.[21]

Proximity was useful for our ancestors, but it can be problematic in the modern world. Society has replaced tigers with chocolate cake. You might be successful in resisting cake . . . until that cake is directly in front of you, a close proximity that intensifies your craving so much that you abandon any prior commitment to eat healthy.

Another problem is ambiguity. Your inner voice will often justify emotional decisions. Are these excuses valid? Sometimes, yes. Sometimes, no. You often conclude that these excuses *are* valid, but it's difficult to know for sure.

Therefore, you need to eliminate proximity and ambiguity in order to resist emotional temptations. Here are some techniques.

Set Exceptions in Advance

Attending a wedding soon? Tell yourself, in advance, whether you *can* or *cannot* eat cake. Make this decision in advance so that you aren't persuaded by the intensified emotions (and potential excuses) that arise later.

Bind Yourself to a Future Decision

The best way to overcome a temptation is to prevent the possibility of surrendering in the first place, sometimes called a *Ulysses Pact*.

This concept originates from the *Odyssey*, a tale in which the hero,

---

[21] Don't forget that spatial distance lies *within* your concept of time. Delivering a speech next week? You will feel the same effect with proximity: The closer your speech, the stronger your emotions.

Odysseus, sails across the sea with his crew. That voyage passed through a dangerous area with mythical creatures, known as Sirens, whose singing was so tantalizing that it drove sailors into a crazy mental state, eventually causing them to crash their boats. Many sailors, blinded by overconfidence, believed that they possessed enough willpower to sail through the area without succumbing.

Those sailors died.

Odysseus was smarter—although he wanted to hear the song, he recognized his shortcomings. He asked every crewmember to place wax in their ears to block the song, and he asked those crewmembers to tie his body to the mast so that he would be incapable of enacting his temptations while hearing the song. If he escaped, they were ordered to attack him.

You can follow the same strategy to resist temptations. You might *believe* that you possess enough willpower to resist a future temptation, yet the shrinking proximity will intensify your emotions, eradicating any stockpile of willpower. Enforce these decisions *before* that moment arrives, while your emotions are less intense. Bind yourself to the outcome so that you *can't* change this decision even when you see the temptation.

Some examples:

- **Leave Your Computer at Work.** Want to spend time with your family after work? But you can't resist surfing the web? Leave your laptop at the office so that you can't succumb to this temptation.
- **Freeze Your Credit Cards.** Literally. Some people curb their spending by freezing their cards in ice. They need to wait for the ice to melt in order to buy something.
- **Publicize Your Goals.** After posting your goals on social media, slacking off becomes less feasible.
- **Write a Teaser Blurb.** At the end of a blog post, describe the post that you'll write next week. Now you're committed.
- **Ask For a Takeout Box Beforehand.** Before a meal, ask the server to place half inside a to-go container so that—when the food arrives—you are less tempted to eat it all.

Ulysses pacts can help you overcome temptations, but they might reduce your enjoyment, too. Remember how rewards dilute your enjoyment? The same effect happens here. Suddenly you are performing these behaviors because you *need* to do them, not because you *enjoy* them. Use this technique at your discretion.

∞

Before ending this chapter, let's see the broader implications in society.

In most movies, villains are fully aware that they are, indeed, the bad guy. But in real life, there are no villains. Everybody believes they are the hero of their personal movie. The abusive spouse. The corrupt politician. The armed robber. They retain this hero status because they have justified their behavior; their bad actions have been balanced.

This blamelessness creates a problem in the criminal justice system. Crimes are usually punished with a mishap, like prison. Or an obligation, like community service. Those outcomes balance the criminal misdeed, and we assume—perhaps naively—that everything will be hunky dory afterward.

But do you see the problem?

Many people have already justified their misdeeds; their equity scale was already balanced. But now, prison *is* dislodging this equilibrium.

Consider a troubled youth, let's call him Paul, who started selling drugs as a teenager. Born into a poor and abusive household, Paul faced an enormous mishap in life. He believes, and perhaps rightly so, that the system failed him. If anything, his crimes were *necessary* to attain a minuscule quality of life. Paul's life was full of mishaps and obligations, so his equity scale was leaning toward the right.

And now society imprisons Paul.

This imprisonment—a large mishap—is *further* tilting his scale to the right, intensifying the imbalance in his scale, giving him more immunity for misdeeds. Prison is *fueling* his criminal behavior. Not resolving it.

Obviously, the issue is more complicated. We still need to hold people accountable for their behavior, and we still need to protect society from dangerous individuals, but hopefully this framework can spark new applications for these systemic issues.

We need a system that won't fail people in the first place. We need to make sure that people, like Paul, can pursue options outside of a criminal path. If they see alternative options, yet they deliberately choose a criminal path, then perhaps prison would become a viable solution because it *would* counterbalance their behavior. However, this situation (i.e., the availability of alternatives) might be few and far between.

And hopefully more research will uncover whether physiological balance is the culprit behind these urges. Imagine if humans lived in a world without any sensations of balance, a world in which we never felt a back-and-forth compulsion. How would society look? If somebody hurt us, would we still feel an urge to hurt this person to correct this imbalance? Or would the lust for revenge magically disappear? And what about fairness? If we didn't feel a craving for physical balance, would we still imprison people, in hopes of correcting whatever imbalance they committed? Or would abstract balance disappear without sensory balance breathing life into this idea?

Sensory concepts—motion, grouping, balance, and more—lie in the deepest abyss of our brain, providing frameworks that guide our behavior in everyday life. These sensory principles escape our conscious awareness, yet they structure the very nature of society. Hopefully this book will spark more research into these ideas.

SUMMARY OF BALANCE

You balance your behavior. When you perform good behaviors, you gain immunity to perform bad behaviors; when you perform bad behaviors; you feel pressured to perform good behaviors.

Keep a Visible Record of Your Indulgence

Your brain will try to erase the memory of a misdeed. Don't let this happen. Eating chocolate? Keep wrappers on the table so that your brain sees the true extent of your misdeed (Polivy et al., 1986).

Force Yourself to Monitor Performance

We face an *ostrich problem*: We deliberately ignore metrics that show negative feedback (Webb, Chang, & Benn, 2013). Eating a lot? You don't weigh yourself. Eating sweets? You don't check your blood glucose. Spending a lot of money? You don't check your balance. If you don't see this negative feedback, then—technically—is it a misdeed? Remind yourself that, yes indeed, your behavior *is* a misdeed. Force yourself to monitor these metrics so that you can't plead ignorant.

Write Short Emails When You Need a Reply

Sending cold emails to people? Write a short email. Like, *really* short. If your recipients see a long email, they might feel obligated to write an equally long email for balance. Plus, a short email gets confused with minimal work in replying: *Hmm, how long will it take to reply? Something feels small. It won't take long.* Once they reply, *then* you can steer the conversation to the intended topic.

Conclusion

NOW THAT WE HAVE journeyed inside the brain, let's rise to the surface so that we can put everything together.

In the Preface, you reflected on reasons for buying this book: *I bought this book because . . .*

   . . . it seems interesting.

   . . . it was on sale.

   . . . I enjoyed his other books.

   . . . my friend recommended it.

But you didn't buy this book for those reasons. You bought this book because you could imagine buying this book. Your conscious reasons may have strengthened this mental picture, but the final decision was based on the ease and vividness of this mental image.

Every decision follows the same process: You imagine the outcome, and then you judge the desirability of it. If this image feels vivid and pleasant, then you move forward with the decision.

Open any book on persuasion, and you'll find an endless arsenal of principles that influence decisions; it can be overwhelming. Yet mental pictures, in my opinion, are the most powerful tool. Mental pictures are the final gatekeeper of any decision. All other principles are feeding into these mental pictures; those principles influence your decisions *because* they influence the mental picture.

Next time that you need to motivate or persuade somebody, don't fixate on individual principles: what to say, how to say it, where to say it. Fixate on the mental picture: How can I make this behavior easier and more vivid? When you focus on this goal, everything else—what to say, how to say it, where to say it—will fall into place.

∞

Let's summarize this book in a unique way.

At this moment, you are probably feeling overwhelmed with so many techniques, unsure where to begin. You would probably benefit from a case study that applies all of the major principles from this book.

So, let's try something unusual.

Think of somebody in your life—friend, colleague, family member—that would gain value from reading this book.

Thinking of someone?

If this person would benefit their life by reading this book, then why not motivate this person to grab a copy? Not only would you be helping them, but you'd also be helping me spread the word about this book. And it would give you a chance to apply these techniques in a real-life scenario. If you hated this book, then use these suggestions to recommend another book.

Let's review each chapter for examples:

- ▶ **Chapter 1: Vividness.** You would need to get this person to imagine buying and reading this book. Any vividness will be largely based on the intensity of your recommendation.
- ▶ **Chapter 2: Physical Ability.** Don't just recommend the book. Send a link to the Amazon page, which will ease their ability to buy it.
- ▶ **Chapter 3: Body State.** If this person doesn't buy things via their phone, then don't send a text. Send an email. They might open this email on their computer (where they *can* imagine buying it).
- ▶ **Chapter 4: Activation.** Keep your email focused on a single topic: this book. Mixing other topics will dilute the activation of this goal.
- ▶ **Chapter 5: Habits.** Why would your friend read it? Enjoyment? Send your email during the weekend, a time period that cues their

enjoyment. Practicality? Send your email during the middle of a workday when they possess a rational mindset.

▶ **Chapter 6: Motion.** Have they read similar books? Mention these other books. You will be reminding them of their momentum in this domain; they won't be starting from scratch.

▶ **Chapter 7: Grouping.** This person should be "close" to you so that you both reside in the same group. If you enjoyed this book, they should enjoy it, too.

▶ **Chapter 8: Balance.** This book isn't a misdeed, so there is nothing to balance. And if it were a misdeed, then you shouldn't be encouraging this person. Use balancing for your own decisions.

The gist: Think of somebody close to you that would enjoy this book, and send this person (and anyone else) an email with a link to the Amazon page. You'd be helping me spread the word, and I'd be really grateful.

Where to Next?

WANT TO STAY updated on my future books? I rarely post on social media, but I occasionally send emails when I think of something interesting to share. I try to make every email worthwhile to read. You can subscribe here:

www.NickKolenda.com

Appendix A

Societal Applications

THIS BOOK FOCUSED on mental pictures in the context of motivation, but the mechanism applies to *any* decision. This Appendix will discuss a few societal applications to illustrate the breadth of this idea.

Discrimination

Read this passage:

> This morning a father and his son were driving along the motorway to work, when they were involved in a horrible accident. The father was killed and the son was quickly driven to the hospital severely injured. When the boy was taken into the hospital a passing surgeon exclaimed: 'Oh my god, that is my son!' (Reynolds, Garnham, & Oakhill, 2006, p. 890).

Were you confused by that passage? So, too, were participants in that study. Gender stereotypes are so ingrained that we sometimes forget that surgeons can also be mothers.

We need to dissociate roles and genders because these associations can lead to discrimination. If the mere title of "surgeon" activates a mental picture of a man, then hiring managers will imagine hiring a man for this job more easily.

Some people scoff at discrimination because they don't see it first-hand. And they're right; most decent people never say: *I'm not going to hire this person because she's a woman.* We never hear those reasons, so we're quick to assume that discrimination doesn't exist. Yet these biases are problematic because they occur below our conscious awareness, even in people who try (and believe they are) fair and unprejudiced.

The same effects occur with racial biases, too. Refer to *The Tangled Mind* for more examples.

Empathy

You empathize via Gestalt principles (e.g., similarity, proximity, enclosure). If you see somebody similar to you, then—much like in the sensory world—your brain groups you and this person as a single entity. You care for this person because you *are* this person.

First, we need research to confirm this idea. I asked a few prominent researchers, and they all agreed that this idea seems plausible and probable. Empirical support would validate the idea and lead to new applications.

For example, in schools, we often tell bullies to be nicer to other kids. But perhaps we overlooking a hidden culprit of low self-esteem. If bullies dislike themselves, then they will inject this dislike into other people. Before you can care for other people, you first need to care about yourself.

Or perhaps we could improve school curriculums. Some parents scoff at classes, like art or music, because these classes seem impractical. Yet those classes might improve the proficiency of sensory grouping. Could skills in sensory grouping improve abstract grouping, like empathy? Perhaps these classes are cultivating more empathy in children.

Goal Motion

Spatial distance is the sensory building block for goal distance. Your brain envisions a goal (e.g., save $2,000) as a point in the distance, a distance that you need to traverse with motion. Anything that affects these sensory concepts (e.g., distance, motion) will affect this mental imagery.

But we're creeping into dangerous territory.

Some people have trouble with spatial motion (e.g., obesity, disabilities, old age). These people perceive spatial landmarks to be farther away because their mental pictures of the traversal are weaker (Sugovic, Turk, & Witt, 2013).

Is this spatial effect entering the abstract domain? Would future events (e.g., next week) or goals (e.g., save $2,000) seem farther away for these people? Could bodily constraints (e.g., obesity, disabilities, old age) reduce motivation for *any* goal, even goals that are unrelated to health or physicality?

As much as I want to hide a possibly painful truth, this outcome might be plausible. And we need more research to investigate this issue.[22]

Or consider the reverse. What if you *eased* spatial motion? For example, spatial landmarks seem closer for people sitting in a car because the traversal seems easier (Moeller, Zoppke, & Frings, 2016). Therefore, would a goal—an abstract concept in the distance—seem closer and easier to achieve while sitting in a fast-moving car?

We should also consider the *type* of motion. Suppose that you are driving on an empty highway, covering a lot of distance with minimal effort. Would a goal seem easier to achieve during this moment?

Or how about these environments:

▶ **Treadmill.** Running on a treadmill requires a lot of effortful motion without any tangible progress. During this sensation,

---

[22] Thankfully, I don't think this detriment would occur. Mental pictures are relative to personal experience. If you suddenly become paralyzed, then yes—you will likely become demotivated because your new spatial motion will be weaker than your familiar motion. But over time, your brain will establish a new baseline of motion.

would any goal seem fruitless, as if you would be working tirelessly without any progress?

▶ **Side Streets.** Left turn here. Then a roundabout here. Then a right turn. Amidst these twists and turns, would you brainstorm a more convoluted path to reach your goal?

▶ **Subway.** If your body is moving sideways on a train, as if you are being pulled by an external force, would you feel less in control with your goal pursuit?

Visualization

It's not really a societal application, but I wanted to clarify a distinction between mental pictures and visualization.

Every self-help guru has uttered these words: *In order to be successful, you need to visualize success.* And I realize that my book title—Imagine Reading This Book—seems to support that statement. But take heed. In this book, the term "mental picture" has referred to the imagery that you construct *during* a decision. Visualization usually occurs outside of these immediate decisions.

Visualizations *can* be motivating, but this strategy has a few issues. For one, your brain has trouble distinguishing between visualization and real life. Right now, imagine eating a handful of M&Ms; envision the sweet taste, as the chocolate melts in your mouth. During this visualization, your brain believes that you are actually eating M&Ms.

Now, what happens when you eat chocolate in real life? You become full, don't you? Or you satisfy your sweet tooth? Well . . . that happens from your mental picture. When participants imagined eating M&Ms, they ate fewer pieces of chocolate from a real bowl because their visualization satisfied their desire (Morewedge, Huh, & Vosgerau, 2010).

That blurring of reality complicates the advice to visualize success: If you imagine yourself succeeding, then it feels like you already succeeded. In that case, why work hard? You don't need to.

Some researchers argue that you can resolve this issue by visualizing *behaviors* (e.g., studying) instead of the *outcome* (e.g., good grade). But this approach still doesn't solve the problem: If you imagine yourself studying, then it feels like you already studied. Why study again?

Plus, you can grow tired of these activities. If you repeatedly imagine reading this book, then you might become less inclined to read it: *Hmm, do I want to read this book? Not really. It feels like I've already been reading it.*

Vision boards and visualization *can* help, but you should limit this technique to two situations:

> ▶ **Visualize to Enhance Performance.** Don't use visualization to motivate yourself. You will only grow tired of this behavior. Instead, use visualization to enhance your performance on tasks, like an upcoming speech. Your speech will be better because, according to your brain, you will have already performed it many times. Visualizations are especially helpful for motor behaviors (e.g., tennis, piano, golf) because your mental practice feels like real practice. If you never grow tired of these activities, then visualize them all you want.

> ▶ **Visualize Unrealistic Goals.** If you can't imagine yourself reaching a goal, then perhaps repeated visualizations could help you transform this vague goal into a vivid and realistic endeavor, which could motivate you.

Appendix B

Everyday Applications

THIS BOOK DISCUSSED a lot of applications, but the possibilities are endless. Here are some new applications for various scenarios. Hopefully they inspire you to brainstorm your own ideas.

Dieting

- ▶ **Keep Healthy Food Readily Available.** Whenever you want food, you want it *now*. The problem? Most accessible foods (e.g., chips, cookies, crackers) are unhealthy. You can imagine eating these foods, but you can't imagine the required work to cook something healthy. Therefore, increase your *ability* to eat healthy food by keeping a fully replenished stockpile of healthy options that can satisfy immediate cravings.
- ▶ **Tie a Red String to Your Fridge Handle.** Every time that you open the fridge, this string will remind you of your original promise and commitment.
- ▶ **Talk to Your Boss.** In Chapter 5, you overindulged on ice cream because you had a rough day at work. Is this a recurring habit? Perhaps these indulgences are the tip of a deeper iceberg. Talk to your boss to resolve any stressful cues at work so that you are solving the problem (not just the symptom).

Exercise

▶ **Find a Logical Cue.** How often do you want to exercise? Find a recurring cue in your life that matches this quantity. I want to exercise every weekday, so I choose a cue that occurs every weekday (e.g., the first moment that I feel mentally depleted in the morning).

▶ **Attach a Small Amount of Exercise.** Once you find a cue, start with a negligible amount of exercise, like a few pushups. Aim for the highest quantity of exercise that doesn't feel like work.

▶ **Choose Exercises That You Enjoy.** I hate running, so I don't run. I love kickboxing, so I kickbox. Don't choose an exercise simply because it seems "standard." Choose exercises that you enjoy so that you prevent negative emotions from creeping into this behavior.

▶ **Pursue This Goal Alone.** An accountability buddy *can* be helpful, but it can also backfire. Each time that you exercise, your brain will associate this person with exercise. If this person stops going, you will be relinquishing all of this pent-up activation, and your motivation will suffer.

Waking Up

▶ **Let Sunlight into Your Bedroom.** Remove any black curtains so that sunlight bursts into your room each morning, inhibiting your ability to sleep.

▶ **Start a Fun Morning Ritual.** Start your day with something fun and enjoyable, like a delicious breakfast or foot massage. Your mental picture of leaving bed will become stronger.

▶ **Sleep in a Higher Bed Frame.** It can be difficult to leave a bed that is lower to the floor: You need to start from a crouching position and push yourself up into a standing position. Higher bed frames are easier to leave; you just tilt your body over the edge into a position that is already standing.

▶ **Wake Up at the Same Time.** A consistent sleep schedule will train your body to wake up at the same time. Waking up will become more activated and imaginable.

Daily Schedule

▶ **Adhere to a Consistent Schedule.** You arrive to work and begin pondering: *Hmm, what should I start working on?* You choose a task, and then an hour later: *Okay, what now?* These choices are harmful because they deplete your motivation (Vohs et al., 2014). Aim to create a consistent schedule so that you eliminate these superfluous decisions. Plus, this consistency will strengthen cues and behaviors. If you consistently eat lunch and *then* read industry news, your brain will build a stronger connection between "lunch" and "industry news." The latter behavior will become easier to imagine because of the heightened activation.

▶ **Number Your To-Do List.** You could eliminate superfluous choices (e.g., which task to do next) by numbering your to-do list. In one study, customers in a loyalty program needed to buy six flavors of yogurt: banana, apple, strawberry, orange, mango, grape. Customers were more likely to finish this task if they needed to buy flavors in a particular sequence (vs. customers who could buy the yogurts in *any* order; Jin, Huang, & Zhang, 2013).

▶ **Ease Future Progress During Downtimes.** Feeling motivated? Yet nothing to do? Make progress on future tasks, like cutting vegetables for dinner that night. When you eventually start this task, your endowed progress will make it easier to resume.

▶ **Don't Procrastinate Via Productivity.** Not all motion is created equal. You might need to file your taxes, but your brain is telling you that you need to vacuum the house, even though—deep down—you know that you *should* be filing your taxes. Your brain is craving motion, and it's trying to trick you with vacuuming because this action seems like forward motion.

Writing Your Goals

▶ **Writing ≠ Progress.** Every self-help guru has uttered these words: *Write your goals.* But does it really work? Or is it another meaningless mantra? Turns out, writing *can* help . . . with a caveat: Writing your goals can't feel like work (see Harkin et al., 2016). If this planning feels effortful, then your brain will use this task as an excuse to procrastinate: "I wrote my goals. Therefore, I don't need to exercise today because I already made progress." Just because you're spending time and effort doesn't mean that you're making progress.

▶ **Avoid Detailed Plans for Difficult Goals.** Planning is especially detrimental with big or difficult goals (Harkin et al., 2016). A big goal, like earning $1 million, can be highly motivating, but the translation of those steps onto paper (and the "holy $#!%" reaction at the amount of work) can deflate your enthusiasm. In one study, overweight people were less likely to diet if they planned their food intake for the day. Upon realizing this difficulty, they gave up: *Oh man, eating healthy is going to be difficult. Why bother?* They were more likely to eat healthy if they *didn't* plan their food intake, thanks to this blissful ignorance.

▶ **Write Your Goals in a Permanent Format.** If you *do* write your goals, maybe skip the half-crumbled sticky note, which can easily be destroyed. Write your goals in a way that will prevent an easy surrender: laminate your goals, tattoo a quote, or publicize your journey on social media.

▶ **Bulleted Lists for Novices . . . Numbered Lists for Experts.** Flexibility entices people to pursue a goal, while rigidity keeps them motivated. Fitness trainers could tweak the list of exercises they send clients. Bulleted lists will be more effective for new clients because, if these exercises can be done in any order, this flexibility will make the fitness goal seem easier to achieve. Numbered lists, on the other hand, will be more effective for expert clients because this rigidity will narrow their focus toward a single path.

Productivity

▶ **Hide the Apps on Your Phone.** Getting distracted whenever you open your phone? Don't keep apps on your home screen; move them so that you need to swipe to reach them. This lack of visibility will prevent these apps from triggering a distraction.

▶ **Delete Tabs From Your Browser.** Can't stop scrolling Twitter or Facebook? Remove those tabs in your browser to inhibit your ability to visit these sites.[23]

▶ **Use a Foldable Room Divider.** My home office is situated next to my living room, a space filled with tempting cues (e.g., TV, couch, video games). If I see those cues, then my brain will imagine those pleasurable behaviors. Sometimes I use a physical boundary (foldable room divider) to block those cues.

Rewards

▶ **Obscure the Reward.** Rewards are detrimental because they siphon activation away from your enjoyment: If you are performing a behavior so that you can receive a reward, then you aren't performing this behavior because you enjoy it. Perhaps you could reduce this dilution by making rewards more ambiguous. Vague

---

[23] Or follow my strategy. Keep 500,000 tabs open . . . then you'll have trouble visiting any single tab.

rewards are less defined, so this lack of clarity might prevent some dilution. The next two strategies might help.

▶ **Obscure the Magnitude.** Researchers offered participants a challenge: Drink 1.4 liters of water in 2 minutes. They enticed some people with a reward of $2, and they enticed other people with a coinflip between $1 or $2. Economically, a certain $2 should have motivated more people, yet only 43% of people completed this task for $2, whereas a whopping 70% of people completed this task for a chance between $1 or $2 (Shen, Fishbach, & Hsee, 2015). This ambiguous reward nearly doubled the number of people who completed the challenge. When giving rewards, try obscuring the exact size: spin a wheel; describe a mystery bonus; randomly select a handful of people.

▶ **Obscure the Delivery.** Slot machines are addictive because you don't know when the next reward is coming. Your brain releases more dopamine, a key neurotransmitter in motivation, while *anticipating* a reward. Your brain will release more dopamine if the reward can occur at *any* moment. Therefore, don't reward people after a fixed interval (e.g., losing 5 lbs.). Reward them after a random interval (e.g., losing 3 lbs. or 5 lbs. or 7 lbs.).

Advertisements

▶ **Show Various Usage Contexts.** You see this strategy in infomercials. Tired of being cold? Yet restricted under a blanket? This blanket has holes. Wear it at home. While watching TV. On the phone. Doing homework. Eating lunch. At a sports game. You conclude: *Oh, I can see myself using it very often. I guess I'll buy it.*

▶ **Don't Skip Steps.** Advertisements often ask you to "buy" a product (e.g., "Buy on Amazon"). But at these early stages, viewers don't possess enough information to envision the purchase. Most ads should emphasize the next step (e.g., "View on Amazon").

▶ **Emphasize a Specialty.** Imagine that you see three brands of toothpaste with different functions: (a) teeth whitening; (b) cavity protection; (c) teeth whitening *and* cavity protection. Brand C *should* be the winner . . . if persuasive were additive. In reality, Brand C seems weaker because of the diluted activation between those two benefits (Chernev, 2007). Many businesses escape this problem by creating separate brands; each brand allows them to emphasize a unique specialty, consolidating activation into a single benefit or function.

Sales Page

▶ **Use Minimal Graphic Design.** Any element on your web page is an element that is diluting activation from the desired action. Reduce the colors, images, and peripheral context to the most minimal form that still looks beautiful.

▶ **Place Entry Points Above the Fold.** Position your headline at the top of the page so that visitors possess the ability to start reading without scrolling.

▶ **Display a Verb of the Intended Action.** When you read verbs, like "touch," your brain activates the muscles responsible for this behavior (see Glenberg & Kaschak, 2002). Clever web designers could nudge you to click a button by using the word "click" inside the button. This text will activate the muscles involved with clicking, which could ease your mental picture of clicking.

Checkout

▶ **Remove Escape Paths.** Amazon removes all of the extraneous links from their checkout. You can't imagine yourself leaving. You can only move in a single direction: forward.

▶ **Hide Unrelated Products.** Suppose that a customer reached the online checkout while buying an outfit for work. Some market-ers will entice this customer by showing related products (e.g., similar outfits). And that's fine. But if these adjacent products are unrelated (e.g., wireless speakers), customers will be less likely to complete the checkout (Friedman, Savary, & Dhar, 2018). Irrele-vant goals dilute the activation of the primary goal.

▶ **Use Rejection Tasks to Anchor Ownership.** Instead of asking people to add optional features, you could ask them which features they *don't* want. In one study, some participants were given a blank car, and they added optional features. Other people were given a fully-loaded car, and they removed features that they didn't want. The latter increased sales because people felt more ownership of features and kept them (Levav et al., 2010).

Sharing on Social Media

▶ **Specify the Network.** Asking people to share on "social media" is vague. Choose a website that seems most relevant and consolidate the activation into this single goal.

▶ **Provide an Example Message.** Without a message, people will be left wondering what to say (and their mental picture of sharing will be weaker).

▶ **Display a GIF Animation.** Don't show a logo of the social network. Show a GIF animation of the message being shared on this network, which is the exact image that recipients need to imagine.

Oh, and also . . .

IF YOU ENJOYED this book, you might enjoy my other books:

- ▶ **Methods of Persuasion (2012).** It's a fun summary of existing research on behavior.
- ▶ **The Tangled Mind (2019).** I crammed all of the research on sensory concepts into *The Tangled Mind*. That book expands on the sensory mechanisms in a lot more detail, but it still has the same quirky flair.

Or do you prefer video content? For the past few years, I've been filming videos that apply my research in various contexts (e.g., web design, pricing, selling). It's now a sizable collection with 15+ hours of tutorials. Just click the "Courses" section on my website: www.NickKolenda.com.

References

Alter, A. L., & Oppenheimer, D. M. (2006). Predicting short-term stock fluctuations by using processing fluency. *Proceedings of the National Academy of Sciences*, 103(24), 9369–9372.

Alter, A. L., & Oppenheimer, D. M. (2008). Effects of fluency on psychological distance and mental construal (or why New York is a large city, but New York is a civilized jungle). *Psychological Science*, 19(2), 161–167.

Bar, M., & Neta, M. (2006). Humans prefer curved visual objects. *Psychological science*, 17(8), 645–648.

Bastian, B., Jetten, J., & Fasoli, F. (2011). Cleansing the soul by hurting the flesh: The guilt-reducing effect of pain. *Psychological Science*, 22(3), 334.

Bélanger, J. J., Schori-Eyal, N., Pica, G., Kruglanski, A. W., & Lafrenière, M. A. (2015). The "more is less" effect in equifinal structures: Alternative means reduce the intensity and quality of motivation. *Journal of Experimental Social Psychology*, 60, 93–102.

Benartzi, S., & Thaler, R. H. (2001). Naive diversification strategies in defined contribution saving plans. *American Economic Review*, 91(1), 79–98.

Berger, J. (2016). *Contagious: Why things catch on*. Simon and Schuster.

Berger, J., & Fitzsimons, G. (2008). Dogs on the street, pumas on your feet: How cues in the environment influence product evaluation and choice. *Journal of Marketing Research*, 45(1), 1–14.

Bhalla, M., & Proffitt, D. R. (1999). Visual–motor recalibration in geographical slant perception. *Journal of experimental psychology: Human perception and performance*, 25(4), 1076.

Brasel, S. A., & Gips, J. (2014). Tablets, touchscreens, and touchpads: How varying touch interfaces trigger psychological ownership and endowment. *Journal of Consumer Psychology*, 24(2), 226–233.

Brasel, S. A., & Gips, J. (2015). Interface psychology: touchscreens change attribute importance, decision criteria, and behavior in online choice. *Cyberpsychology, Behavior, and Social Networking*, 18(9), 534–538.

Camerer, C., Babcock, L., Loewenstein, G., & Thaler, R. (1997). Labor supply of New York City cabdrivers: One day at a time. *The Quarterly Journal of Economics*, 112(2), 407–441.

Cameron, J., Banko, K. M., & Pierce, W. D. (2001). Pervasive negative effects of rewards on intrinsic motivation: The myth continues. *The Behavior Analyst*, 24(1), 1–44.

Caruso, E. M., Van Boven, L., Chin, M., & Ward, A. (2013). The temporal Doppler effect: When the future feels closer than the past. *Psychological science*, 24(4), 530–536.

Castro, D. C., Samuels, M., & Harman, A. E. (2013). Growing healthy kids: a community garden–based obesity prevention program. *American journal of preventive medicine*, 44(3), S193–S199.

Chang, H. H., & Tuan Pham, M. (2013). Affect as a decision-making system of the present. *Journal of Consumer Research*, 40(1), 42–63.

Chartrand, T. L., & Bargh, J. A. (1999). The chameleon effect: the perception–behavior link and social interaction. *Journal of personality and social psychology*, 76(6), 893.

Chernev, A. (2007). Jack of all trades or master of one? Product differentiation and compensatory reasoning in consumer choice. *Journal of Consumer Research*, 33(4), 430–444.

Cialdini, R. B. (2007). Influence: The psychology of persuasion. New York, NY: Collins.

Cian, L., Krishna, A., & Elder, R. S. (2015). A sign of things to come: behavioral change through dynamic iconography. *Journal of Consumer Research*, 41(6), 1426–1446.

Coulter, K. S., & Coulter, R. A. (2005). Size does matter: The effects of magnitude representation congruency on price perceptions and purchase likelihood. *Journal of Consumer Psychology*, 15(1), 64–76.

Davidai, S., Gilovich, T., & Ross, L. D. (2012). The meaning of default options for potential organ donors. *Proceedings of the National Academy of Sciences*, 109(38), 15201–15205.

Davis, S. N. (2003). Sex stereotypes in commercials targeted toward children: A content analysis. *Sociological Spectrum*, 23(4), 407–424.

Deci, E. L., Koestner, R., & Ryan, R. M. (1999). A meta-analytic review of experiments examining the effects of extrinsic rewards on intrinsic motivation. *Psychological bulletin*, 125(6), 627.

Dong, P., Huang, X., & Wyer Jr, R. S. (2013). The illusion of saving face: How people symbolically cope with embarrassment. *Psychological science*, 24(10), 2005–2012.

Elder, R. S., & Krishna, A. (2012). The "visual depiction effect" in advertising: Facilitating embodied mental simulation through product orientation. *Journal of Consumer Research*, 38(6), 988–1003.

Etkin, J. (2016). The hidden cost of personal quantification. *Journal of Consumer Research*, 42(6), 967–984.

Etkin, J., & Ratner, R. K. (2012). The dynamic impact of variety among means on motivation. *Journal of Consumer Research*, 38(6), 1076–1092.

Fishbach, A., & Zhang, Y. (2008). Together or apart: When goals and temptations complement versus compete. *Journal of personality and social psychology*, 94(4), 547.

Fogg, B. J. (2019). Tiny Habits: The Small Changes That Change Everything. Houghton Mifflin Harcourt.

Forest, A. L., Kille, D. R., Wood, J. V., & Stehouwer, L. R. (2015). Turbulent times, rocky relationships: Relational consequences of experiencing physical instability. *Psychological science*, 26(8), 1261–1271.

Friedman, E. M., Savary, J., & Dhar, R. (2018). Apples, Oranges, and Erasers: The Effect of Considering Similar versus Dissimilar Alternatives on Purchase Decisions. *Journal of Consumer Research*, 45(4), 725–742.

Gal, D., & McShane, B. B. (2012). Can small victories help win the war? Evidence from consumer debt management. *Journal of Marketing Research*, 49(4), 487–501.

Gibson, J. J. (1979). The ecological approach to visual perception. *Psychology Press*.

Gino, F., Norton, M. I., & Ariely, D. (2010). The counterfeit self: The deceptive costs of faking it. Psychological science, 21(5), 712–720.

Glenberg, A. M., & Kaschak, M. P. (2002). Grounding language in action. *Psychonomic bulletin & review*, 9(3), 558–565.

Gollwitzer, P. M., & Brandstätter, V. (1997). Implementation intentions and effective goal pursuit. *Journal of personality and social psychology*, 73(1), 186.

Gneezy, U., & Rustichini, A. (2000). A fine is a price. The Journal of Legal Studies, 29(1), 1–17.

Gregory, W. L., Cialdini, R. B., & Carpenter, K. M. (1982). Self-relevant scenarios as mediators of likelihood estimates and compliance: Does imagining make it so?. *Journal of personality and social psychology*, 43(1), 89.

Gross, J., Woelbert, E., & Strobel, M. (2015). The fox and the grapes—how physical constraints affect value-based decision making. *PloS one*, 10(6).

Gu, Y., Botti, S., & Faro, D. (2013). Turning the page: The impact of choice closure on satisfaction. *Journal of Consumer Research*, 40(2), 268–283.

Hamilton, M. C., Anderson, D., Broaddus, M., & Young, K. (2006). Gender stereotyping and under-representation of female characters in 200 popular children's picture books: A twenty-first century update. *Sex Roles*, 55(11–12), 757–765.

Harkin, B., Webb, T. L., Chang, B. P., Prestwich, A., Conner, M., Kellar, I., . . . & Sheeran, P. (2016). Does monitoring goal progress promote goal attainment? A meta-analysis of the experimental evidence. *Psychological bulletin*, 142(2), 198.

Harrison, M. A., & Hall, A. E. (2010). Anthropomorphism, empathy, and perceived communicative ability vary with phylogenetic relatedness to humans. *Journal of Social, Evolutionary, and Cultural Psychology*, 4(1), 34.

Huang, X. I., Dong, P., & Wyer Jr, R. S. (2017). Competing for attention: The effects of jealousy on preference for attention-grabbing products. *Journal of Consumer Psychology*, 27(2), 171–181.

Huang, L., Galinsky, A. D., Gruenfeld, D. H., & Guillory, L. E. (2011). Powerful postures versus powerful roles: Which is the proximate correlate of thought and behavior?. Psychological Science, 22(1), 95–102.

Jin, L., Huang, S. C., & Zhang, Y. (2013). The unexpected positive impact of fixed structures on goal completion. *Journal of Consumer Research*, 40(4), 711–725.

Jin, L., Xu, Q., & Zhang, Y. (2015). Climbing the Wrong Ladder: The Mismatch Between Consumers' Preference for Subgoal Sequences and Actual Goal Performance. *Journal of Marketing Research*, 52(5), 616–628.

Judge, T. A., & Cable, D. M. (2004). The effect of physical height on workplace success and income: preliminary test of a theoretical model. *Journal of Applied Psychology*, 89(3), 428.

Kahneman, D., Knetsch, J. L., & Thaler, R. H. (1990). Experimental tests of the endowment effect and the Coase theorem. *Journal of Political Economy*, 98(6), 1325–1348.

Kang, C. (2013, September 1). Google crunches data on munching in office. Retrieved June 16, 2020, from https://www.washingtonpost.com/business/technology/google -crunches-data-on-munching-in-office/2013/09/01/3902b444-0e83-11e3-85b6 -d27422650fd5_story.html

Karmarkar, U. R., & Bollinger, B. (2015). BYOB: How bringing your own shopping bags leads to treating yourself and the environment. *Journal of Marketing*, 79(4), 1–15.

Kille, D. R., Forest, A. L., & Wood, J. V. (2013). Tall, dark, and stable: Embodiment motivates mate selection preferences. *Psychological Science*, 24(1), 112–114.

King, D., & Janiszewski, C. (2011). The sources and consequences of the fluent processing of numbers. *Journal of Marketing Research*, 48(2), 327–341.

Kronrod, A., Grinstein, A., & Wathieu, L. (2012). Enjoy! Hedonic consumption and compliance with assertive messages. *Journal of Consumer Research*, 39(1), 51–61.

Lee, H., Fujita, K., Deng, X., & Unnava, H. R. (2017). The role of temporal distance on the color of future-directed imagery: A construal-level perspective. *Journal of Consumer Research*, 43(5), 707–725.

Lee, A. Y., & Labroo, A. A. (2004). The effect of conceptual and perceptual fluency on brand evaluation. *Journal of Marketing Research*, 41(2), 151–165.

Lev-Ari, S., & Keysar, B. (2010). Why don't we believe non-native speakers? The influence of accent on credibility. *Journal of experimental social psychology*, 46(6), 1093–1096.

Levav, J., Heitmann, M., Herrmann, A., & Iyengar, S. S. (2010). Order in product customization decisions: Evidence from field experiments. *Journal of Political Economy*, 118(2), 274–299.

Loersch, C., Aarts, H., Payne, B. K., & Jefferis, V. E. (2008). The influence of social groups on goal contagion. *Journal of Experimental Social Psychology*, 44(6), 1555–1558.

Maimaran, M., & Fishbach, A. (2014). If it's useful and you know it, do you eat? Preschoolers refrain from instrumental food. *Journal of Consumer Research*, 41(3), 642–655.

Maglio, S. J., & Polman, E. (2014). Spatial orientation shrinks and expands psychological distance. *Psychological science*, 25(7), 1345–1352.

Mandler, J. M. (2004). *The foundations of mind: Origins of conceptual thought*. Oxford University Press.

Mazar, N., Mochon, D., & Ariely, D. (2018). If you are going to pay within the next 24 hours, press 1: automatic planning prompt reduces credit card delinquency. *Journal of Consumer Psychology*, 28(3), 466–476.

Moeller, B., Zoppke, H., & Frings, C. (2016). What a car does to your perception: Distance evaluations differ from within and outside of a car. *Psychonomic bulletin & review*, 23(3), 781–788.

Morales, A. C., & Fitzsimons, G. J. (2007). Product contagion: Changing consumer evaluations through physical contact with "disgusting" products. *Journal of Marketing Research*, 44(2), 272–283.

Morewedge, C. K., Huh, Y. E., & Vosgerau, J. (2010). Thought for food: Imagined consumption reduces actual consumption. *Science*, 330(6010), 1530–1533.

Mishra, A., & Mishra, H. (2010). Border bias: The belief that state borders can protect against disasters. *Psychological science*, 21(11), 1582–1586.

Mishra, H., Mishra, A., & Nayakankuppam, D. (2010). How salary receipt affects consumers' regulatory motivations and product preferences. Journal of Marketing, 74(5), 93–103.

Mukhopadhyay, A., & Johar, G. V. (2009). Indulgence as self-reward for prior shopping restraint: A justification-based mechanism. *Journal of Consumer Psychology*, 19(3), 334–345.

Mulatti, C., Treccani, B., & Job, R. (2014). The role of the sound of objects in object identification: evidence from picture naming. *Frontiers in psychology*, 5, 1139.

Napolitano, C. M., & Freund, A. M. (2017). First evidence for "The backup plan paradox." *Journal of Experimental Psychology: General*, 146(8), 1189.

Neal, D. T., Wood, W., Lally, P., & Wu, M. (2009). Do habits depend on goals? Perceived versus actual role of goals in habit performance. Manuscript under review.

North, A. C., Hargreaves, D. J., & McKendrick, J. (1999). The influence of in-store music on wine selections. *Journal of Applied Psychology*, 84(2), 271.

Norton, M. I., Mochon, D., & Ariely, D. (2012). The IKEA effect: When labor leads to love. *Journal of consumer psychology*, 22(3), 453–460.

Nunes, J. C., & Drèze, X. (2006). The endowed progress effect: How artificial advancement increases effort. *Journal of Consumer Research*, 32(4), 504–512.

Phillips, W., & Boroditsky, L. (2003). Can quirks of grammar affect the way you think? Grammatical gender and object concepts. In *Proceedings of the Annual Meeting of the Cognitive Science Society* (Vol. 25, No. 25).

Polivy, J., Herman, C. P., Hackett, R., & Kuleshnyk, I. (1986). The effects of self-attention and public attention on eating in restrained and unrestrained subjects. *Journal of personality and social psychology*, 50(6), 1253.

Reber, R., & Schwarz, N. (1999). Effects of perceptual fluency on judgments of truth. *Consciousness and cognition*, 8(3), 338–342.

Redden, J. P. (2008). Reducing satiation: The role of categorization level. *Journal of Consumer Research*, 34(5), 624–634.

Reynolds, D. J., Garnham, A., & Oakhill, J. (2006). Evidence of immediate activation of gender information from a social role name. *The Quarterly Journal of Experimental Psychology*, 59(05), 886–903.

Riener, C. R., Stefanucci, J. K., Proffitt, D. R., & Clore, G. (2011). An effect of mood on the perception of geographical slant. *Cognition and Emotion*, 25(1), 174–182.

Schnall, S., Zadra, J. R., & Proffitt, D. R. (2010). Direct evidence for the economy of action: Glucose and the perception of geographical slant. *Perception*, 39(4), 464–482.

Schneider, I. K., Eerland, A., van Harreveld, F., Rotteveel, M., van der Pligt, J., Van der Stoep, N., & Zwaan, R. A. (2013). One way and the other: The bidirectional relationship between ambivalence and body movement. *Psychological Science*, 24(3), 319–325.

Scott, M. L., & Nowlis, S. M. (2013). The effect of goal specificity on consumer goal reengagement. *Journal of Consumer Research*, 40(3), 444–459.

Sela, A., & Berger, J. (2012). How attribute quantity influences option choice. *Journal of Marketing Research*, 49(6), 942–953.

Shen, L., Fishbach, A., & Hsee, C. K. (2015). The motivating-uncertainty effect: Uncertainty increases resource investment in the process of reward pursuit. *Journal of Consumer Research*, 41(5), 1301–1315.

Shen, H., & Sengupta, J. (2014). The crossmodal effect of attention on preferences: Facilitation versus impairment. *Journal of Consumer Research*, 40(5), 885–903.

Shiv, B., & Fedorikhin, A. (1999). Heart and mind in conflict: The interplay of affect and cognition in consumer decision making. *Journal of consumer Research*, 26(3), 278–292.

Soman, D., & Cheema, A. (2004). When goals are counterproductive: The effects of violation of a behavioral goal on subsequent performance. *Journal of Consumer Research*, 31(1), 52–62.

Soman, D., & Zhao, M. (2011). The fewer the better: Number of goals and savings behavior. *Journal of Marketing Research*, 48(6), 944–957.

Song, H., & Schwarz, N. (2008). If it's hard to read, it's hard to do: Processing fluency affects effort prediction and motivation. *Psychological Science*, 19(10), 986–988.

Strahilevitz, M., & Myers, J. G. (1998). Donations to charity as purchase incentives: How well they work may depend on what you are trying to sell. *Journal of Consumer Research*, 24(4), 434–446.

Sugovic, M., & Witt, J. K. (2013). An older view on distance perception: Older adults perceive walkable extents as farther. *Experimental Brain Research*, 226(3), 383–391.

Sugovic, M., Turk, P., & Witt, J. K. (2016). Perceived distance and obesity: It's what you weigh, not what you think. *Acta psychologica*, 165, 1–8.

Taylor, J. E. T., & Witt, J. K. (2010). When walls are no longer barriers: Perception of obstacle height in parkour. *Journal of Vision*, 10(7), 1017–1017.

Tu, Y., & Soman, D. (2014). The categorization of time and its impact on task initiation. *Journal of Consumer Research*, 41(3), 810–822.

Valins, S. (1966). Cognitive effects of false heart-rate feedback. *Journal of personality and social psychology*, 4(4), 400.

Van Kerckhove, A., & Pandelaere, M. (2018). Why are you swiping right? The impact of product orientation on swiping responses. *Journal of Consumer Research*, 45(3), 633–647.

Vohs, K. D., Baumeister, R. F., Schmeichel, B. J., Twenge, J. M., Nelson, N. M., & Tice, D. M. (2008). Making Choices Impairs Subsequent Self-Control: A Limited-Resource Account of Decision Making, Self-Regulation, and Active Initiative. *Journal of Personality and Social Psychology*, 94(5), 883–898.

Webb, T. L., Chang, B. P., & Benn, Y. (2013). 'The Ostrich Problem': Motivated avoidance or rejection of information about goal progress. *Social and Personality Psychology Compass*, 7(11), 794–807.

Wells, G. L., & Petty, R. E. (1980). The effects of overt head movements on persuasion: Compatibility and incompatibility of responses. *Basic and applied social psychology*, 1(3), 219–230.

Witt, J. K., Proffitt, D. R., & Epstein, W. (2005). Tool use affects perceived distance, but only when you intend to use it. *Journal of experimental psychology: Human perception and performance*, 31(5), 880.

Wolf, J. R., Arkes, H. R., & Muhanna, W. A. (2008). The power of touch: An examination of the effect of duration of physical contact on the valuation of objects. *Judgment and Decision Making*, 3(6), 476.

Xu, A. J., Schwarz, N., & Wyer, R. S. (2015). Hunger promotes acquisition of nonfood objects. *Proceedings of the National Academy of Sciences*, 112(9), 2688–2692.

Xu, A. J., & Wyer Jr, R. S. (2008). The comparative mind-set: From animal comparisons to increased purchase intentions. *Psychological Science*, 19(9), 859–864.

Zhang, Y., Fishbach, A., & Dhar, R. (2007). When thinking beats doing: The role of optimistic expectations in goal-based choice. *Journal of Consumer Research*, 34(4), 567–578.

Zhang, Y., Fishbach, A., & Kruglanski, A. W. (2007). The dilution model: How additional goals undermine the perceived instrumentality of a shared path. *Journal of personality and social psychology*, 92(3), 389.

Zhao, M., Lee, L., & Soman, D. (2012). Crossing the virtual boundary: The effect of task-irrelevant environmental cues on task implementation. *Psychological Science*, 23(10), 1200–1207.

Zwaan, R. A., & Taylor, L. J. (2006). Seeing, acting, understanding: Motor resonance in language comprehension. *Journal of Experimental Psychology: General*, 135(1), 1.